ARE YOU READY FOR SUCCESS?

Ida Greene, Ph.D.

ISBN 1-881165-02-7
Library of Congress Card Catalog Number: 96-93089

ATTENTION COLLEGES AND UNIVERSITIES, CORPORATIONS, AND PROFESSIONAL ORGANIZATIONS:
Quantity discounts are available on bulk purchases of this book for educational training purposes, fund raising, or gift giving. For information contact:
P. S. I. Publishers, 2910 Baily Ave. San Diego, CA 92105 (619) 262-9951.

ACKNOWLEDGEMENTS

I Wish To Thank The Following:

My mother who encouraged me to get an education, and my father who showed me how to be an entrepreneur, both are deceased.

In Pensacola, Florida where I grew up, I thank, my fifth and sixth grade teacher, Mrs. Bascom; my eighth grade teacher, Mrs. Ragland; tenth, eleventh and twelfth grade teacher; Mrs. E. B. Debose, all who saw my potential before I was aware of it.

My college advisor, Dr. I.N. McCollom, for helping me to stretch beyond my limitations to reach for higher goals, and to God for implanting within me a spirit of power, courage and a sound mind.

Ida Greene

Since the first publication of this book, April 14,1991, Ida Greene, Ph.D., RN, Marriage, Family, Child Counselor has established Our Place Center Of Self-Esteem, a non-profit organization that assists children, and families to cope with issues of abuse. A portion from the sale of each book is donated to Our Place Center Of Self-Esteem. Dr. Ida Greene speaks, conduct seminars, and workshops on personal/professional growth topics, (619) 262-9951.

Other books by Dr. Ida Greene:
Light the Fire Within You,
Soft Power Negotiation Skills™,
How to Be A Success In Business,
How To Improve Self-Esteem In The African American Child.

Audio Cassette tapes::
Money, How to Get, How To Keep It,
Light The Fire Within You.

Video Cassette:
Self-Esteem, The Essence Of You.

The Road to Success

I believe there is a natural impulse within all creation to evolve, expand and refine itself; we either stagnate and die or better ourselves and live, more productive and fuller lives. All of nature tells us to change and evolve; notice the leaves on a tree as they move from a flower blossom to a leaf, and the seasons of the year as they go from cool to warm and wet to dry. Nothing ever remains the same including our body which works continuously to digest, assimilate and maintain a state of normalcy regardless of the kinds of food we eat.

There is a peculiar characteristic about us humans that makes us want to better our condition and improve our lifestyle. God has implanted within us a striving to be more, to strive for completion and wholeness; the foundation on which is self-esteem, self-confidence and faith in a power greater than ourselves. Many of us seek to make changes in our outer lives yet fail to listen to our inner prompting. Yet there are others who only want to eat, sleep, and live a life of quiet desperation, futility, hopelessness, and helplessness. We were born to pro- create and create, to improve our life and the lives of others through the accomplishment of our dreams and aspirations in life. When we become better, those around us become better also. Therefore, it is in the best interest of society, for all of us to want more out of life, to strive to improve our life and the lives of those around us. This is what success is all about. Success is the progressive realization of a worthwhile goal and the attainment of that goal. When we are actively pursuing a goal it brings joy, hope and excitement into our lives. There is an exhilaration of love, compassion and understanding for others. It all begins with us helping ourselves.

However we must feel worthwhile and deserving of something better in life for it to become a reality in our life. The road to success is beset with obstacles and seeming challenges. This is good, for it gives us an opportunity to employ the principles of faith, hope and confidence.

Maybe you are thinking that success is for a chosen few and you are not one of them. If this is your thinking, begin now to erase that idea from your mind. Success is a natural state of being for all. There are three types of success- personal, spiritual, and financial. You will need to decide what type of success is right for you at this point in your life. It may be personal success, where you work on your relationships with others; spiritual success, whereby you decide if there is a Supreme Power in the universe and discover your relationship to that power. On the other hand, you may need an improvement of your material success, so you can better provide for your family's daily needs or give more financially to your church or favorite charity. Whatever the reason, success awaits you, it is your natural heritage and right, to want more and to want to improve the lives of other.

Many of us would rather do anything but improve our financial circumstances. There is a perception that to have money involves hard work and a denial of pleasure. What it will require is you to take action to make your dreams become a reality. For you to experience more money or success in life, it will require you to: increase your faith factor, have a strong belief in a divine benevolent power to sustain and support you, be willing to do all you are humanly able to do, know when to let go so that God can guide you in the right direction, be open to miracles and know that there is nothing that God can't do. You must be willing to learn and grow emotionally, intellectually, and spiritually. Also you will need to change any negative mental programming you have about money and success. Say to yourself "money is a tool I can use, to improve the quality of life for others and myself."

"Am I Ready for Success?"
(How to Glide through the Success Maze)

INTRODUCTION

This book is dedicated to the female entrepreneur, the future leader of tomorrow. The world desperately calls you forth. It needs your ingenuity, intuition, compassion, caring nature, love, and sense of justice. The world needs you to guide it, as mankind embarks on the age of high technology, computers, machinery, space travel, mass communication, and guided missiles.

Even though this book is dedicated to the female entrepreneur, men as well as women must work together to create a new world order, one that draws upon the strengths of both sexes to create a loving, caring, humane society where no one is inferior nor superior to another. The principles for success stated in this book will work for you whether you are male or female.

In the past, women stood in the background and functioned as a resource and support for the male figure. Many women discounted their judgment, their intellect and have held enabling, inferior beliefs about themselves and other women. They were told they did not use critical thinking skills to solve problems, and they were too emotional to handle tough challenges. Many women and men believed that in the past, and some still do today. While it is true that women often rely on their intuition, and feelings to solve problems- it is also true that women use their intellect to problem solve in complex situations. What diversity! A creative person is someone who uses both intellect and intuition in a problem solving endeavor to arrive at a decision. Women, creative? I will bet you have never heard women described as being creative. Is it possible that both women and men, have viewed women in a negative manner? I venture to say, yes.

It does no good to blame anyone for this oversight. And, it is an oversight. Women are awakening. They are no longer in a dream state. They are learning they have value, and have an important contribution to make to our society. All people are unique, and all play a vital role in the making, and keeping of a nation, regardless of gender.

CONTENTS

Chapter 1

How to Glide Through the Success Maze

We are all light-bearers. We must all begin to let our light shine, women as well as men. Women are people who display love, intuition, compassion, ingenuity, a caring nature, and a sense of justice. Women must lead mankind to a new level of integrity, and personal interaction. Women must take with them the weapons of compassion, honesty, justice, truth, faith, love, right action, and peace as they interact with other human beings at home and abroad.

Likewise, it is time to take action, my brother. It is time to take action, my dear sisters. The world seeks your ideas and opinions. Believe in yourself. Believe in the goodness of all people. Seek to develop the best in yourself. Know that both women and men can be leaders.

Choose today, to be a light leader. To be a leader of light demands you stay closely in touch with your inner spiritual self and blend it with your intellectual, social, emotional self to become a new creature. A person who is both human and divine. And, who operates from this frame of reference on a continuous basis. Not everyone can be a light leader, will you be the one? Are you ready for success?

Success is not a something-for-nothing activity. Nothing in life is free. Jesus paid with His life for salvation. You will have to pay a price for everything you get in life including success. If you do nothing, nor aspire for nothing in life; you will be one of the scorned, the beggars, or a person who has no control over his or her destiny. You will be one who is at the mercy of others; who looks to others to provide for you, and supply your daily needs. God gave mankind dominion over the earth and all therein. You can not take dominion from a lowered mind

1

set. You must take a step up in your consciousness (thinking); to elevate your thoughts on a higher plane, so you are on a level with the greater good you seek. All good things in life are created from a divine, Christ-like state of mind. All things must be created through our cooperation with God, the union of our mind with the mind of God, and the subordination of our will to the will of God. The only power you and I have is the power we use, through our connection with, and union to God. We, humans cannot create anything. However, we can be co-creators with God, if we understand and use the tools of spiritual intuition/revelation, be reverent, obedient, and humble to this "Greater Force/Higher Power," I call God. God created this earth, and all therein, and God is in control of all living species on the planet. We were created by God in It's (His) image and likeness.

We are God's creation. We came from God, therefore we are one with God. We are a physical and spiritual child of God. Just as an egg is a part of a chicken, we likewise are a part of God. We are the human manifestation of God. We are not "The God." We are the little "I." God is the big "I," the supreme "Power." Everything that has breath is under the ruler ship of this "Supreme Power and Force," and stands obedient to this "Force," I refer to as God. We cannot create a sperm or an ovum. We can not create life nor can we keep ourselves alive forever. No one escapes death but God. He who is in control of life and death has all power, and is all powerful.

God is eternal and lives throughout all generations. However, if you live in obedience to God's laws, work within and use these laws, you can create wonders. You must always remember that there is the Big God and the little God (human beings), whom God created in His image. The minute you think you are greater than God and do not need God, you place a wedge between you and God, and your path of self-destruction will begin. God will allow you to have many growth experiences, until you learn to put things in proper perspective.

2

The lesson we humans have to learn and understand is "that every knee shall bend and every head shall bow in obedience to this power-force-law-principle," I call God. You can use all that God created in the universe for your pleasure as long as you remember that it is the "Father's good pleasure to give you (us) the kingdom of heaven (on earth)." This means we can have all the desires of our heart as long as we do not take from the good of another, and what we create, benefits others as well as ourselves. God will not allow us to be selfish and prosper for long. For in the blink of an eye everything we have created can be destroyed.

If we have faith and look to God as the supplier of our ideas, desires, and aspirations we can have all we want, and more. We only need to understand and remember God's second commandment to us, "Thou shalt have no other gods before me." We can never make a God of, or worship our possessions. We come into this life with nothing, and we depart with nothing.

All that we accumulate on our journey through life is our experiences, memories, emotional growth, and spiritual enlightenment to help complete our spiritual growth and end the birth to death cycle.

It is through our desires and goals we become motivated to change the circumstances in our life. Everything we achieve in life begins with a desire to excel and achieve. Our desire/s is an idea. An idea is a thought or a group of thoughts. It is an image or a picture in your mind. Napoleon Hill stated in the book Think and Grow Rich, "whatever the mind can conceive and believe it will achieve."

When you make a decision to have or create your thoughts/desires it then becomes a goal. All goals can be achieved through a plan of action. This plan of action is what I call success. Success is anything you desire to have, to be or want to do. The following diagram shows you what you need to do to achieve success.

Desire   to   Excel   →Goal   Directness   →Energy/Vitality →Enthusiasm →Fire/Light →Joy, Happiness, Love = Aliveness

Answer the questions below to help prepare you to be open to new ideas and opportunities for success:

1. Are you currently doing the kind of work that adds pleasure to your life, or are you bored and stuck into survival issues to earn a living or prepare for your future?

2. What goal(s) would give you energy, drive or desire to achieve?

3. What do you need to do to create a sense of urgency, to take a new path in life or work on a new goal?

4. If there were no barriers in your life, what would you be, do, or have? Where would you live? Let yourself daydream for a moment before you write your answers.

Basic Truths About Success
Our word does not have to act, it is acted upon. Therefore it is our business to know the Truth, and the Truth's business is to produce the result.
— ERNEST HOLMES

He who binds himself to a Joy Doth the winged life destroy; but he who kisses the Joy as it flies Lives in Eternity's sunrise.
— WILLIAM BLAKE

TEST YOUR SUCCESS POTENTIAL

1. Although I think a lot about success, I don't think I will totally succeed. True__ False__

2. I find it necessary to exaggerate about my performance in order to let people know my strengths, or how good I am. Frequently__ Sometimes__ Never__

3. It is possible for me to be successful in One__ Some__ All areas of my life__.

4. Although, I am content with my life, I am liable to find myself thinking about what someone else has achieved. Often__ Sometimes__ Never

5. I equate success with money and/or power. Yes__ Partially__ No__

6. I have written goals for myself. Yes__ No__

7. I consistently evaluate myself. Yes__ No__

8. I have enough self-discipline to reorganize and redirect, if I find myself getting off track. Yes__ No__

9. I find myself thinking more about what success is than how I will get there. Always__ Sometimes__ No__

10. My potential to succeed is a reality. I am where I want to be True__ False__

Chapter 2

ARE YOU READY FOR SUCCESS?

What is Success? Success is whatever you want it to be. Success is your ability to dream or imagine something in your mind, and to then create that in the physical realm; from the un-manifest to the manifest. Success is any dream, desire, goals you long for and eventually achieve. Your desires may be personal, professional, spiritual or a combination of all you desire. We are by nature, goal seeking, goal striving individuals. If we are not seeking ways to improve ourselves on a personal, professional and spiritual level, decay of the mind sets in, and we begin to die slowly.

It is the nature of the human species to evolve, improve, and perfect its flaws or deficiencies. When this does not happen stagnation occurs in our physiological system, in the form of disease, slow degeneration and cell destruction until all the cells in our body no longer gives off energy or light. We then return to our original form of dust, "ashes to ashes and dust to dust."

The natural progression of the human species is birth → goal seeker/goal striving → movement → energy → excitement → enthusiasm → aliveness → light → contentment → love → joy → bliss → peace with oneself, one's God and all species on planet earth → end of reincarnation → eternal life.

The unnatural progression of the human species is birth → unhealthy living is anger, hostility, chemical/ substance/ emotional/ physical abuse, fear, low self-worth/ esteem/ confidence, lack, limitation, lack of faith in God/ Supreme Being/ isolation/ aloneness/ no spiritual support, confusion → lack of trust in others → disorganization → destruction → apathy → emotional death → physiological death → disintegration → reincarnation to learn unlearned lessons and end the birth to death cycle of life.

Are You Ready for Success?

What you are is God's gift to you. What you make of yourself is your gift to God. On the basis of this premise answer the following question below. Write whatever comes to your mind, do not write what you think someone wants you to say or what you think God wants you to say or to do. Write a brief sentence for each question. Write quickly, do not contemplate whether your answers are right or wrong.

1. What does success mean to you?

2. What is your earliest memory of wanting to achieve or accomplish?

3. Who are your role models or whom do you admire?

4. What would you like to do, become, or have?

5. What would it take for you to be happy in life?

6. Define happiness for you.

7. Since we were created to be goal striving, achieving human beings, what contribution will you make for the betterment of mankind before you die?

8. Sit down in a quiet place close your eyes and go over the same questions in your mind. And again write whatever comes to mind.

To determine your quality/degree of life, answer the following questions to help you diagnose where you are on the continuum of birth → life to death, or life to life cycle.

1. Do you have a dream, or longing, you would like to achieve?

   What is it?

2. Is this a wish or a longing?

3. What is the difference to you between a wish, dream or longing/goal?

4. How will you decide what you really want out of life?

5. How do/will you decide between conflicting goals/dreams?

6. Has anyone in your family ever set a goal/s to do something, and accomplished it?

7. If your answer to the above is no, how will you develop a desire to achieve, or complete a goal if no one in your family has done the process to make a wish, or dream be a reality?

8. How will you acquire a drive to achieve your goal/s?

9. What aspect of your character will you need to develop that may be dormant or non existent? e.g. achiever, positive outlook, faith, stick-to-itness, motivation, drive etc.

10. Is the amount of money you make your indicator of success? If not what is your indicator of successful completion of a goal/success?

11. Do you feel it is unchristian to desire success, be successful, or have money?

12. Do you feel money is the "root of all evil," or the evil use of money is the "root of evil"?

13. Have you decided what you really want out of life or is what you want someone else's idea of what would be best for you to do?

14. How long will it take you to complete your goal/s or obtain your desired success?

15. Have you figured out how to start, so your goa becomes real?

    a.   What is the first thing you will do to get started? List each step of your plan, from step 1 to step 5. Write down now what you will do and how you will proceed. E.g. Decide on a short term goal I can complete in 30 days. These are the thing I will do to make my dream a reality. I will do the following steps:

        1. I will –

        2. I will –

        3. I will –

        4. I will –

        5. I will –

b. Now go through the same process for your intermediate goal/s (90 days to 1 year.)

1. I will –

2. I will –

3. I will –

4. I will –

5. I will –

c. Now go through the same process for your long range goal/s (5–10 years).
1. I will –

2. I will –

3. I will –

4. I will –

5. I will –

16. How will you stay focused on your dream/goal?

17. How will you handle setbacks or disappointment?

God does not cause bad things to happen to us. God works through us by changing our consciousness (mind set), and our heart. God never does anything to us or for us. We create our hardships, disappointments and bad luck through our negative thought patterns and our lack of faith that *God is our refuge and strength, a very present help in trouble. –* PSALMS 46:1

Words of Wisdom

The great end of life is not knowledge, but action.
– THOMAS HENRY HUXLEY

They that seek the Lord shall not want any good thing
– PSALM 34:10

Chapter 3

DO YOU REALLY WANT SUCCESS?

Do you really want success? Are you totally committed to your dream? What goal or objective would you like to achieve, but think is unlikely?

Well, *Dust Off* those old dreams. It is time to daydream again. Just as you did when you were a child. Remember when you believed in magic? You thought it, believed it, it happened.

Let's pretend again. It is time to let yourself digress in time to age 5, or 6, the age of magic. Somewhere between the ages of two and nine, magical things seemed to happen all the time. Let's take a journey back in time, momentarily in your memory, to a time when you did not have a fear of power, fear of success, fear of failure, fear of identity loss, fear of having too much money or not enough, fear of being different, fear of disapproval, nor a fear of not being liked or accepted.

What happened between the age of nine and your mid-twenties? Who stole your dreams? Who told you that your ideas were foolish, that they could never happen, and even more importantly, you could not accomplish your "far-out" dreams? Was it an overcautious parent, or yourself who feared you might experience rejection or ridicule? Was it a shortsighted friend or acquaintance? Did you think that the mind stopped growing with the body? Who taught you how to be so cautious? Dreams are the healthy infant, who lives inside us, and if properly nurtured with desire, develop into a passion for achievement, and success.

There are many steps along the path to success. If our thoughts are infected with caution and doubt, we get the forerunner of worry to fears. Then we experience fear of achievement, fear of failure, fear of success, low self-esteem and low self-confidence.

Fear inhibits our efforts to achieve our desires and dreams. We want to achieve but, we hear a little voice inside of us that says, "can you do it?" You have to say yes to the doubting voice. If the answer inside of you says "I'm not sure," more than likely you will never achieve your dream without some guidance to help you move through your own manufactured fears of success. Your dreams eventually fade away and die if they are not fueled with desire or expectation of accomplishment. Without ever knowing why, you begin to feel empty, hollow, lack energy, drive or enthusiasm. If this has happened to you, that is alright. You can start anew today. I hope this book will nudge you to get started, and work through the barriers you have allowed to come between you, and the successful completion of your dreams and goals.

Success *means different things to different people*. Success to you may mean losing ten pounds of unwanted weight; to another individual who is a single parent it may mean making enough money to feed and clothe three children. Yet to another woman it may mean making $50,000 a year. While to a homemaker whose children no longer need her, it may signal her transition into the work force for the first time to experience a different kind of success. To a homemaker, success may mean finding a job that will make her feel "needed" again. To a man success may have a different meaning.

What unfulfilled need/wants do you have, that are prodding you to do something different with your life? Why do you want to accomplish something or feel successful? Whatever you define as success, it will entail that you take a risk. Success entails taking risks, ability to get things done, and the right use of power.

My definition of success is the ability and willingness to take risks, to reach a goal or objective. And, the ability to use power in a judicious manner.

16

Power is the ability to make a decision and follow through with it regardless of the consequences. Power is situational and is relative to the task before you. The kind of power available to us and the way we use power, will vary depending upon the situation, circumstances, and perceived status of the person involved in the interaction. The key factor in the use of power is to act, or decide without hesitation.

Most women are taught as little girls to defer decision-making to the male of the family. However, this is inconsistent with the assumption of leadership or promoting confidence in one's ability to be the head of household. Often, if the home is a single-parent female household, one of two things may happen. Decisions are made jointly by the female authority figure with outside male input, or decisions are made by the male child with the parent figure relinquishing her power and leadership role in the family to the male child due to a perceived notion that she does not have power, or that only men know how to exert power. If the latter occur, the child gets to have and use power he or she is ill equipped to handle. The child is allowed to assume the role of the adult and misses the opportunity to be a child, and/or to learn from an adult role model effective coping skills to handle life stressors.

Whenever power is placed in the hands of those who are emotionally ill-equipped to use it, the situation is similar to a misguided missile, that becomes dangerous because it wanders aimlessly off its path. If we assume the role and responsibilities of power and leadership authority, we may find ourselves acting child like, and forgetting to take action or we may abdicate our power and leadership role. Also, if we make a blunder in the decision-making process, and are criticized for it, we will grow up with a fear of decision-making and a fear of power because it was associated with a negative outcome.

Many female children see either males making decisions and using power or if they see a female using power, the female authority figure is often uncomfortable and unsure of herself and longs for a

17

male partner to assist her in this role.

Most women could benefit from a course in the uses of power and decision making. You will need these skills whether you desire success or not. Stop right now, Take a journey within. Then ask yourself, Am I ready for success?

Are you ready for success? There are some basic fears you will need to overcome as you embark on your journey to success. The first fear is a Fear of Power.

Fear of Power is a major challenge for women, because they have learned to associate power with the male gender rather than the female. Therefore, when many women have a chance to use power, or are in a powerful position they emulate the male behavior, for that position. They fail to modify or feminize their position. So they become confused in their role identity and uncomfortable in their body; because of incongruence between what they are doing and how they perceive themselves. Power is situational. It is always affected by one's gender.

A female in a position of authority does not need to act like a male. If she is secure in her role as an authority figure, she only needs to request or command and if her wishes are not obeyed she needs to have a way to reinforce her commands, and authority so they are carried out by those under her leadership.

Power is not power if one does not have the ability to reinforce one's position of command, or if it is unheeded by those under its command. Most people respect authority and positions of authority. However, there are a few individuals who like to challenge authority figures. If you should ever find yourself in this position, you will need to confront the individual to resolve the matter swiftly and effectively. Otherwise, it can act as a smoldering flame, which if ignored will be to your disadvantage.

Power not used or misused is just a bad as no power at all. Power must be used in a judicious manner to serve and benefit all parties. The next fear to master is the fear of being different.

Fear of being different. This fear ties closely with a fear of power. To be a woman is to be different, just as it is different to be a man. It is great to be a woman, to be an African-American, to be An A Jewish, Japanese, Chinese, Asian, A Puerto Rican, short, tall, fat, skinny, to speak with an accent, etc. These are qualities that enhance our beauty and individuality. Others will only see these qualities as a problem if you do. Acknowledge that you are different, which is wonderful and get on with the tasks before you.

Fear of not being liked or accepted is a problem only if you allow it to become one. The truth of the matter is that not everyone will like you. Many people hate themselves, so it stands to reason that they will hold you in the same esteem as they do themselves. Just accept that you will not please everyone, and that not all people will like you, for reasons only they know the answer. Just accept it as a fact of life and get on with the business of living your life from integrity and purpose. Seek to get people's respect, not their affection.

If people respect the decision you make, that is enough. The decision you make in their regard may not please them and that is O.K. You are not in a popularity contest to see how many people like or dislike you. You are in your job to reach the company' objectives and get your job done in the most judicious manner possible. Most times it is not what we say but the way in which we say something that creates conflict between us and others.

Most people can handle negative feedback, if it is given in a tactful manner and presented in the form of a sandwich. We sandwich our negative remarks between two positive statements. To try this, give the person one or two positive compliments, then share the negative feedback and remember to conclude with a positive statement. People always remember the last thing we say to them, so be sure to leave them with a positive image of the words you want them to maintain.

Leadership is a lot like fighting on a battlefield. Our personal interactions do not always turn out as we would like due to the individuality of others perception of our behavior. Our behavior may be

19

interpreted by others as disapproval or acceptance. We may not always win all of the little battles of life. But, if we can leave others with peace in our minds and heart about our interaction with them commend yourself. For human nature does not always follow a pre-scribed course of action.

Fear of Disapproval/Rejection is related to the need to be liked. If you received a fair share of disapproval and or rejection by a parent figure, you may have a sensitivity towards this and you may wrongly interpret a "no" response and criticism as disapproval or rejection. It is wise not to be overly sensitive. As the saying goes, "Don't wear your heart on your sleeves." It is natural that not all people will agree with the ideas and opinions of all people. Isn't that great? The world would be boring without disagreements.

Fear of Failure You may ask yourself, what if I fail? So what if you fall down and skin your knee? Do you stay down on the ground? No, you get up, brush yourself off and continue with your business. We must approach success with the same attitude. Success is not always a straightforward path. You may have to zig-zag along the way. You may take a detour. Or, you may stop at any destination along the way and pause. All is O.K. as long as you remember that you paused and know how to get back on track again. If you need a reminder, here it is! You were only supposed to take a short break in your journey to successfully accomplish your dreams and aspirations. If you have paused too long, it is time now to give yourself a pep talk, reassess the distance before you and work out a road map to success that is sensible and workable for you. Rest if you must, but never give up on yourself. Tell yourself you can do it. Keep plugging along! And eventually you will reach your destination. PLUG ALONG!

Plug Along

It's the steady, constant driving
To the goal to which you're striving
Not the speed with which you travel,
That will make your victory sure;
It's the everlasting gaining,
Without whimper or complaining
At the burdens you are bearing
Or the woes you must endure.
It's the holding to a purpose,
And never giving in,
It's the cutting down the distance
By the little that you win;
It's the iron will to do it,
And the steady sticking to it.
So whate'er your task, go to it!
Keep your grit and plug along!
— ANON.

Fear of Success, never, how could you ever achieve too much, accomplish too much, do or be too much. Most people have the opposite problem. They have not set their heights far enough. They forget to dream and imagine where they could go in their career, or who or what they could become. They see only what is in front of them today, which may be negatively impacted by yesterdays' failures. They forget to set their gaze out into the blue horizons of possibilities to where they could possibly go, do, or become.

The mind needs a visual image reflected upon it through imagining or daydreaming, before it can create a plan to accomplish the things we desire.

No one has ever accomplished a goal, without first visualizing it in their mind and then mapping out a plan to reach their desired goal. Whatever we imagine and ardently desire, we can and will achieve.

There are many books written about visualization. Here is an easy and simple way to utilize visualization techniques to accomplish the things you desire in life. The objective is to use your imagination to conjure a picture in your mind's eye. Go ahead and try this now. This technique will work even if you are not a visual person. First gather all your supplies. You will need a red object. It can be an apple, a red piece of cloth, or an orange object. It can be a shoe, a blouse or a towel. Now let's begin. Become quiet and think about what you want to do. Stare at the red object for approximately 30 seconds. Now close your eyelids. Use your skills of imagery to see if you can picture a visual image of the red object flashing across the screen of your mind. If you can't, continue to practice in this manner until you can see a red object flashing across the screen in your mind's eye. It is O.K. to open your eyes to get a quick peek if the color begins to fade. Do this practice exercise once a day for one week. If you need more time, continue to practice this technique.

After you have mastered this, begin to associate anger, with the red color. Next practice this with the color yellow. Follow the same procedure with the yellow color, except associate the color yellow with the sunshine. Then think of the sunshine and associate the yellow color with happiness.

Now move to the next step of the visualization process. Begin to associate happiness with your new job, promotion, or goals you have outlined for your career. Now get a global picture in your mind's eye about the next step you need to take to move up the career ladder. Now see yourself in a new job position. Become very specific and detailed about what your new job will entail; the location or address of the building, the color of the building and the room.

Imagine the floor in the building where you will be working. Is it on the first floor or the 10th floor over looking the bay? See your name plate with the title on your desk. Imagine the color of the suit you will have on when you go for your interview at the corporation.

See the Executive Manager, welcoming you into the firm, telling you that your salary is exactly what you had envisioned. If you leave out any details, go back over this guideline again. Continue daily to do this exercise until every objective you desire is accomplished.

If you are a doubtful person, who tends to imagine the worst outcome of everything, it will take a little longer for you to see positive results. This is a four-stage process.

First, you have to visualize what you want.

Second, you have to believe it can happen.

Third, you have to believe it can happen to you.

Fourth, you must believe you are deserving of this good.

There is a list of books and an audio cassette tape album in the front of this book that you can order to guide you through this process. Be persistent. Know that other people have reached their goals and why not you? Success is not a destination. It is a journey. The journey you will travel, as you achieve your dreams and goals. The following poem summarizes success.

YOU MUST NOT QUIT

When things go wrong, as they sometimes will, when the road
you're trudging seems all uphill, when the funds are low and the
debts are high, and you want to smile, but you have to sigh, when
care is pressing you down a bit...
Rest if you must, but do not quit.
Life is queer with its twists and turns,
As everyone of us sometimes learns,
And many a fellow turns about when they might have won had they
stuck it out. Don't give up though the pace seems slow...
You might succeed with another blow.
Often the goal is nearer than it seems
To a faint and faltering person; often the struggler has given up
when they might have won the victor's cup; they learned too late

when the night came down, how close they were to the golden
crown. Success is failure turned inside out..the silver tint of the
clouds of doubt, and you never can tell how close you are, it may be
near when it seems afar; so stick to the fight when you are hardest
hit, it's when things seem worst that you must not quit.

– ANON

You are where you are today because of the: thoughts you think, moment by moment, mental image (visualization) you hold about you/your life, expectations you/others have about your ability, and the vision you entertain about your life's purpose. Reverend Michael Beckwith says, visioning is different from visualization; it is a transformation of the human self, into the divine, spiritual self to allow the presence of God to use you. And you do not tell God what to do, nor ask God for anything. You glorify God, by allowing God to express through you, for a "Higher" purpose to serve your fellow man.

I suggest you start with visualization, to train your mind to expect better, a higher good, to achieve your goals. Then shift to the visioning process, as outlined by Michael Beckwith, where you become a master like the great mystics. And allow the universe to use you, by aligning yourself with divine ideas of joy, harmony, love, and wisdom. To do this you will need self-awareness.

Self-Awareness – Is the ability to see yourself as you really are, to accurately assess your own needs, your strong and weak points and areas in which you need to improve. It is easy to think that we are perfect and everyone else needs to improve. We can all become better people. Periodically make out a personal growth chart for yourself, grade yourself on a scale of one to ten. Some of the categories might be "quick temper," "easy going," "hard driver," "relaxed," "cooperative," "stubborn." Do this annually to gauge how much growth you have achieved. For greater effectiveness and to increase your self-awareness have a co-worker and a friend, grade you. Then compare the score you gave yourself to the score that each of them gave you.

24

Salesmanship – All successful entrepreneurs need a course in sales-manship. All of life is about selling. You will need to sell someone on the idea, you are the best person for the job, and that they need to hire you. You may need to sell the people working under you or over you on a new idea you would like to put into effect. You may need to sell your boss on the idea that you deserve a promotion or a salary increase. Do take a class in selling. If nothing else you will learn how to sell you on you. You are a product, and you are a commodity. You have skills and talents. You have value. Will you be undersold? Who will decide how much you are worth?

To move to the top of the success ladder you will need to sell your services and talents and no one knows how valuable you are, but you. Are you worth the effort and time someone would need to pay if they hired you? If you cannot resoundingly say yes to these questions, begin to work on your self-esteem; seek the assistance of profession-als who can help you. Be willing to pay to become a better product (person). Be realistic and honest with yourself. Seek ways to improve yourself. You are a commodity. Are you a Volkswagen or Mercedes Benz? It's all a state of mind. The mind is the creative cause of all that transpires in a person's life. Our personal conditions are the results of our actions and our actions are the results of the thoughts and ideas we think.

IT'S ALL IN THE STATE OF MIND

If you think you are beaten, you are,
If you think you dare not, you don't
If you like to win, but you think you can't
It is almost certain you won't.
If you think you'll lose, you're lost,
For out in the world we find
Success begins with a fellow's will –
It's all in the state of mind.
If you think you are outclassed, you are,

25

You've got to be sure of yourself before
You can ever win a prize.
Life's battles don't always go
To the stronger or faster man,
But soon or late the person who wins
Is the person who thinks they can!
– ANON

Drive to Action – This is where you pull together all of the above traits and characteristics into concrete, realistic, effective action. Whereby you take advantage of the opportunities afforded you and transcend the obstacles before you.

Life in its great and wonderful abundance is pouring itself out to us as unexpected good, in the form of unexpected money.

Affirm by stating out loud, "I now claim for myself…"

A TREATMENT FOR UNEXPECTED MONEY
I am one with the infinite abundance of God.
I know no separation from life.
I am a divine, perfect expression of the One God, which
having created all of Life, continually creates Life.
This Creation is working in and through me, Mind acting
upon Mind, Life acting upon Life.
It lives through me as perfect activity.
Right now I cease to separate myself from God.
I allow good to come into my experience. I let it flow
generously and abundantly.
There is no great or small in the eyes of God.
I am open to receive.
I am accepting divine Good from an Infinite Source.
I am accepting Abundance. I am expecting to prosper.
I am expecting the unexpected.
I have no concern about paying taxes on this money.

I have no concern about paying tithes.
I put up no barriers.
I am open and receptive to the inflow of Good in my Life.
I thank Thee, Father, Source of all Life.
— Reverend Sheila Roberts

If You Can Imagine It, You Can Achieve It,
If You Can Dream It, You Can Become It.
— Kristone

Chapter 4

ARE YOU READY FOR BUSINESS SUCCESS?

The exercises in this section will help you to decide what is your mission in life. It will allow you to assess how far you have come in this process and help you determine if you have the character traits and skills needed to achieve your goal/s. It will teach you how to focus and stay focused so that you can stay motivated with your chosen vision. It will help you to make sense out of all the mumble, jumble, chatter in your mind. You will learn the principles of success and will be able to decide by the end of the quiz if you are a candidate for success.

SELF TEST
Am I Ready for Business Success?

1. I know what I want out of life? Yes_____ No_____

2. Have I chosen a business that blends with my personality, abilities and interests? Yes_____ No_____

3. I know my business strengths and weaknesses and I have taken measures to utilize the services and skills of others to balance my weaknesses. Yes_____ No_____

4. I have accepted that I will need the services of competent professional for my business growth and I am prepared to pay for these services. Yes_____ No_____

5. Do you have financial and quantitative goals set for you and your business?   Yes____ No____
6. Do you have an action plan for accomplishing your goals and are they tied to a time frame?   Yes____ No____

7. Are you self-disciplined?   Yes____ No____

8. Can you work long hours and make sacrifices?
                                                 Yes____ No____

9. Do you have management ability?   Yes____ No____

10. Do you have enough experience in your field?
                                                 Yes____ No____

11. Are your goals realistic and obtainable   Yes____ No____

12. Do you love what you do?   Yes____ No____

13. Is your purpose to own a business clear to you?
                                                 Yes____ No____

Dr. Dorothy Height, president of the National Council of Negro Women when asked, "what makes the great?" stated "Greatness is not measured by what a man or woman accomplishes, but by the opposition he or she overcame to reach his goals."

You can be a success in any business you desire. The Reverend Johnnie Coleman, Pastor of the Christ Universal Complex in Chicago teaches, "You don't have to be sick or broke. You can go within and bring forth the power to change things." Each of us has within us a sleeping giant, which when activated with desire, a strong determination, and unrelenting persistence will eventually melt away the greatest obstacles in our path. Success, whether business or otherwise belongs to the person who will pursue what they desire tenaciously without giving in to despair, set backs, disappointment, tragedy or failure. They achieve success because they never look back with regret at the past, but continue to look ahead to the possibilities of the future. These people have an unshakable faith, and belief in a God that is ready, willing, and able to take care of them, and sustain them through their trials and tribulations.

According to Dr. Hugh Gloster, the past president of Morehouse College, when asked "what made him one of America's one hundred best college presidents?' Replied "You must establish your dreams and quietly move in the direction of attaining them." Much of this has to do with the way we use our mind. In the books, *Working With The Law*, by Raymond Holliwell and *Think And Grow Rich, A Black Choice*, by Dennis Kimbro and Napoleon Hill, the authors discuss mental laws and how the use of them can create wealth.

Everything you see now began as an idea in someone's mind. Your physical world is nothing more than the lingering evidence of that which has already taken place in your mind. It is an extension or out picturing of your thoughts. Yours is a mental world. Raymond Holliwell states, "mental laws are the infrastructure of life." Kimbro states, "Just as one is blinded to physical laws, mental laws are also undetectable to the eye." Thoughts and ideas are living, breathing, things. They are the raw materials from which all that we desire, create, or accomplish in life comes from.

Therefore, right now you are where you are in your business or financial condition because of the thoughts you are thinking. If you desire a change in your business or in your finances, you must examine the quality of thoughts you entertain on an hourly basis. The more you think about lack, bad times, or scarcity, the more these circumstances will appear in your life. William James, the Harvard Psychologist stated, "You are what you think about most of the time." What you think on increases and grows in proportion to the amount of energy thought you feed it. Therefore, if you desire success or wealth, make this your predominant thought for twenty-two hours in a twenty-four-hour day.

To have money or acquire money will require that you increase your prosperity consciousness. And here are some principles that can help you. First, prosperity is a state of mind. As you think, you become. Second, prosperity is a state of mind that results from right thinking. It is the result of your recognition of the nature of your inner being. Your inner self is a creative individual expression of God. Because the nature of God is abundant, and prosperous, when you identify your human nature with your God nature, you see yourself as a child of God. An individualized, creative, expression of God. You were made in the image and likeness of God. Also you came from God and after your stay on earth you return to God. You are the vessel through which God manifest and express. So if the nature of God is prosperous, abundance, wholeness, perfection, and complete, then so are you.

You are not lacking in anything for the perfection, prosperity, abundance, and wholeness, of God to come forth. What is needed is a correction in your thinking and thought patterns. You need to make a shift in your consciousness from lack to abundance, from helpless to hopeful, from an impoverished outlook to a prosperous outlook. Learn to think optimistic, positive and upbeat. Have an unwavering faith in God's ability to provide for your needs. If God can provide for the birds of the air, the fish in the sea, and the worms of the earth, surely God must love you, because he created in his image, enough to provide for you.

Maybe, it is you who has abandoned God, rather than God abandoning you. You have to pray to heal your mind of any belief in fear, lack, or limitation. You must keep your mind on God and the Goodness of God, on a continuous and daily basis. Prosperity is an inner spiritual state of adequacy, abundance, fullness, love, joy, harmony, peace, and forgiveness from harm, or wrong by you or others.

The two emotional states that will mentally prepare you to receive prosperity is gratitude and forgiveness. Affirm daily that your every need is known by God, and supplied before you ask, because God loves you, and knows what you need before you ask. You were not sent to earth to fend for yourself. You are God's child, and God will take care of HIS children. You come through your parents, Physically. They are your human nurturer and protector, but spiritually you belong to God.

Whatever you become in life is the result of your sustained energy and focus over a long period of time. This explains why success is not a straight path. Most of us have a lot of negative mental conditioning and programming that has to be unlearned. This process of change can be likened to having a bucket of dirty water that you want to become clear water. If you replace the dirty water with a bucket full, it will get clear more quickly than if you replace the water with a spoon. However, the rate of change will be proportional to your willingness to give up your old negative thought patterns, your comfortable ways of doing things; to learn a new way of being. And be open to change and grow on a daily or hourly basis. There are many personal and professional success skills you will need to develop, before you achieve proficiency in any new endeavor.

AFFIRM THE PERFECT EXPRESSION OF ABUNDANCE

Prosperity is the nature of perfect Being. Prosperity is a state of mind. Therefore as I think, I become. Prosperity is a state of being that comes from right thinking and can only result from my recognition of the nature of my inner being. I am meant to be successful. My freedom as a creative individualization of God enables me to achieve success in every phase of life. This state of freedom is true spiritual prosperity. Prosperity, received and established in my mind, is automatically manifested in my world.

I have the ability to be my complete, creative, best self at all times, under any circumstance. Prosperity results from my desire and inten-tion to express God in me.

There can be no limit to my prosperity, because God removes all limitation from my consciousness. As I am freed from the bondage of my fears and false beliefs, I experience true manifestation of prayer. My spiritual nature brings me real prosperity. From the center of my inner being all abundance works come forth. I identify myself with the abundance of God, and I am prosperous today.

Today I claim my affluence, abundance, and prosperity. I experi-ence fullness. I claim my good and go where I want to go and do what I want to do as long as it does not interfere with others. I affirm my prosperity. I receive and use money, knowing that it indicates spiritu-al prosperity. I have freedom, and God is expressed fully in me when I am free.

Through my word, I make known to the abundant universe what I want. I individualize the Universal. Whatever I ask, I know I receive.

I LIVE THE FULLNESS OF LIFE, NOW

It is a deep satisfaction to be alive today. I am glad I know who I am and what I am. I am a child of God. It is satisfying to know that everything I do is the action of God within me. I experience the full gratification of every desire, when I make my will one with the Universal will. God working within me satisfies my every demand on the eternal law of perfect self expression. I live at the point of cause, and the effect is complete fulfillment.

My life is the Father's life and is an outlet for his creativity to express through me. I am the focal point in the universal creative mind of God. I am a willing servant, and an open vessel for the Goodness of God to flow through, and so it is.

ESSENTIAL SUCCESS SKILLS

Below are some skills you will need to develop before you are successful in your chosen field. Take this inventory to discover your deficiencies, circle the one's where you need improvement.

Write a statement about what you will do to correct any deficiency or short coming you find. *Underneath each area write the plans you will implement to have mastery in this area*

1. Self-Esteem:
    a. Self-Concept-Identity

    b. Self-Worth

    c. Self-Respect

2. My Self-Image,
    a. Strengths

    b. Shortcomings/weakness

    c. How I appear to others

    d. Handicaps I need to overcome

3. Thing I need to know for my:
   a. Self-Acceptance

   b. Self-Confidence

4. Communication Skills I need to develop:

5. Success Skills, I need to develop or improve –
   a. Clearly defined goals with a time line for completion
   b. Being Responsible
   c. Being Dependable
   d. Being Trustworthy
   e. Being Accountable
   f. Areas above I need to improve:

6. To favorably impress others to get cooperation, I will....

7. Skills I need to improve for success are:
   a. How to dress
   b. How to walk
   c. How to talk
   d. Negotiation skills – Soft Power™
   e. Interview skills for a job
   f. Writing a resume
   g. Talking on the phone – telephone etiquette
   h. Follow up/marketing skills
   i. What I will do about the above:

8. Do your personal assessment now
   I know:
   a. How to cope with rejection
   b. How to accept "NO"
   c. How to stay motivated
   d. How to maintain belief in myself during hardship, disappointment, or failure.
   e. I need help in the above:

I AFFIRM:

I dedicate myself to be of maximum service to God, myself, and those around me; to live in a manner that sets the highest example for others to follow and to remain responsive to God's guidance.

I Go Forth With a Spirit Of Enthusiasm, Excitement and Expectancy. I Am Safe. I Am at Peace.

THE MASTER MIND PRINCIPLES
How To Be Successful In Anything You Do
Form a Master Mind group. It is better to use the success skill of other like-minded persons to reinforce your determination and belief. Your conviction is the key to overcoming any negative belief in anything you do in life. These are the principles of the Master Mind:

1. I SURRENDER

I admit that, of myself, I am powerless to solve my problems, powerless to improve my life.

2. I BELIEVE

I come to believe that a power greater than myself; the Master Mind, can change my life.

3. I AM READY TO BE CHANGED

I realize that erroneous self-defeating thinking is the cause of my situations, unhappiness, fears, and failures. I am ready to change my beliefs and attitudes in order to transform my life.

4. I DECIDE TO BE CHANGED

I make a decision to surrender my will and my life to the Master Mind. I make this change from deep within.

5. I FORGIVE

I forgive myself for all my mistakes and shortcomings. I also forgive all other persons who may have harmed me.

6. I ASK

I make known my specific requests, asking my partners' support, in knowing that the Master Mind is fulfilling my desires now, with every breath I take.

7. I Give Thanks

I give thanks that the Master Mind is responding to my desires, and I assume the same feelings of success now, knowing that all my requests are being fulfilled.

8. I Dedicate My Life

I now have a covenant in which it is agreed that the Master Mind is supplying me with an abundance of all my desires to live a successful, happy, and joyous life.

How to Be a Marketing Guru

Your ability to market yourself and your business is the key to your success or failure in business. Everything revolves around selling in some form. However, marketing is the "life line" of your business, so it is critical that you know the difference between marketing and sale. Marketing should be an on going activity for your business over time. Marketing includes the following:

1. Branding, a brand name, logo and a business tag line that lets others know what you do
2. Business Cards
3. Advertisement
4. Direct mail
5. Speaking
6. Seminars /workshop
7. Direct mail
8. Books, e-books.

On the other hand sales includes the following:
1. Personal Self-Esteem/Self-Image
2. Business Self-Image
3. Success Identity
4. Self-Confidence

5. Management of the following Fears
    a. Fear of Failure
    b. Fear of Success
    c. Fear of Criticism
    d. Fear of Unworthiness
    e. Fear of Money

*When you cannot get a compliment in any other way,
pay yourself one –* MARK TWAIN

*Whatever you do or dream you can do, begin it.
Boldness has genius, power, and magic in it.*
– GOETHE

BIBLICAL QUOTES FOR PROSPERITY

*Let the Lord be magnified, which hath pleasure in the
prosperity of His servant. –* PSALMS 35:27

*Thou openest Thine hand, and satisfiest the desire
of every living thing. –* PSALMS 145:16

Chapter 5

How to Create a Success Self-Image

This section will help you understand the principles of self-motivation, what you must do on a daily basis to stay motivated. So you are able to face the barriers or fears that will surface to block your vitality, and cause you to feel depressed, un-motivated, procrastinate and give up on your dreams. The key, is an improved self-esteem, based on a new self-image.

Your self-esteem is endless, ongoing, it is eternal. It is the essence, of who you are, not what you or others see you as. It is fragile, can be affected by many factors, and needs maintenance on a continual basis. Because the self-esteem you spend months to develop can be destroyed in one minute, by a careless remark, or unkind word. Our self-esteem is the vehicle that gets us to our chosen goals in life. However, the foundation and the fuel that propel us is our self-image.

Each time you change, you create a new you. So your self-image need match the new role you will play. You will never be congruent, until the "play" you, matches the real you.

The things all people need whether or not they want success in their career are:

1. Security; a feeling that one's basis needs for food and shelter is secure. When you have a sense of security, you feel grounded, and important.
2. Acceptance, your identity; you are accepted by both parents as being important to the family unit.
3. Self-Worth (value to family)
4. Self-Esteem, a process where you are esteemed and made to feel

that you count, that you make a difference by your presence in the family unit.

Write down feelings of inadequacy you feel in any of these areas.
1. Security – (Safety)

2. Acceptance – (Identification)

3. Self-Worth – (Value to family/to life)

4. Self-Esteem – (Esteemed/appreciated)

POSITIVE THOUGHTS

The trouble is, if you don't risk anything, you risk even more.
— ERICA JONG

All things work together for good to them that love God
— ROMANS 8:28

I discovered I always have choices and sometimes it's only a choice of attitude. – ABRAHAM LINCOLN

SELF-TEST
PERSONAL SUCCESS INVENTORY

1. I know what I want out of life?   Yes__ No__
2. I have chosen a business that blends with my personality, abilities and interests?   Yes__ No__
3. I know my business strengths and weaknesses. I have taken measures to utilize the services and skills of others who balance my weaknesses.   Yes__ No__
4. I have accepted that I will need the services of competent professionals for my business growth, and I am willing to pay for these services.   Yes__ No__
5. Do you have financial and quantitative goals for yourself and your business?   Yes__ No__
6. Do you have an action plan to accomplish these goals and are they tied to a time frame?   Yes__ No__
7. Are you a self-disciplined person?   Yes__ No__
8. Are you willing to work long hours or sacrifice? Yes__ No__
9. Do you have expertise in your chosen field?   Yes__ No__
10. Do you love doing what you do?   Yes__ No__
11. Is your purpose to own a business clear to you? Yes__ No__
12. Is this career choice your mission in life?   Yes__ No__
13. Do you feel a higher calling to be in business? Yes__ No__

There are no right or wrong answers to this quiz. Your chance of business success increases if you can answer yes to all questions. Retake, this quiz once a month to see how you have progressed.

SELF-ESTEEM – THE ESSENCE OF YOU

To help you discover the unconscious barrier that may be blocking your success, examine your beliefs and attitudes about money and success. Do you see money as "the root of all evil?" How do you feel about wealthy people or people with money? Are they people you like and admire? If you dislike wealthy people, you will never allow yourself to become wealthy, especially if you like yourself now. Because you would have to dislike yourself to become one of the wealthy.

Do the exercises below to help you gain freedom from feelings of low self-worth, and an undeserving mental program. What can you do to improve the aspects of your personality. *State what you will do to create a new you.*

1. My Self-Esteem:
   a. Self-Concept/Identity

   b. Self-Worth

   c. Self-Respect

2. My Self-Image:
   a. My weaknesses

   b. Way I appear to others as

   c. My handicap/s to overcome are

3. My Self Acceptance:
   a. Ability to like myself, as I work to change my faults.

4. My Self-Confidence

5. Communication Skills I need to develop:

6. Listed below are some general character traits needed for success in a business, or position of leadership. Where do you fall on a scale of 1to10 in personal development in these areas? The highest level of proficiency is 10, and the lowest is 1.

   a. Responsible – I am a # __because,

   b. Dependable – I am a # __because,

   c. Trustworthy – I am # __because,

   d. Accountable (accept responsibility for one's mistakes without resorting to justify) – I am a # __because,

POSITIVE THOUGHTS
   God provides the victuals, but He does not cook the meal.
   – ANONYMOUS

   The principal maker of genius is not perfection but originality, the opening of new frontiers. – ARTHUR KOESTLER

Chapter 6

Gliding Through the Corporate Success Maze

The corporate world is the backbone of our great nation. It is a place where one can soar to great heights. It is also a place where you can drop to the depths of despair, so do what you can to make life easier and better for both yourself and your fellowman. Go often to the quiet resources of your inner-self for there is where you will find the power, strength and determination to propel you forward when things go awry.

The world of high technology and the age of the computer is upon us. However, we will always need the resources of talented individuals, such as yourself, to bring ethics to the conglomerate giant—The Business World.

To succeed in the corporate world, you will need to believe in yourself. To know that the world needs you and that you make a difference in the scheme of things. This may not always be apparent to you, for no one will ever say this to you. I am saying this to you now. *I want you to know that you are needed in the business world.* The world needs your input. You provide a piece of the puzzle that no other human being on the face of the earth can supply. You are unique. You are one of a kind among many. The contribution you make may seem insignificant. But who among us can judge. Whatever talent you have to share, *be good at it.*

Know when to push and when to pull. Use wisdom and truth in all of your encounters with others. You have the power to influence others. But the person over whom you have the greatest influence is you. Never allow discouragement and disappointment to linger. There is always tomorrow, and there will always be another opportunity.

Spend time developing your talents, skills and inner resources. You are a product. Are you a marketable product? Always seek to make yourself a better person and a better employee. If you believe in yourself and have a strong belief in a power greater than yourself, you will make it to the top. Use wisdom along the way as you glide through the corporate maze to the top.

Wisdom

Look to this Day, for it is Life-the very Life of Life.
In it's brief course lie all the varieties and realities of your
  existence: the bliss of Growth, the glory of Action, the
  splendor of Beauty.
For yesterday is already a dream and tomorrow is
  only a vision;
but to-day, well-lived, makes every yesterday a dream of
happiness and every to-morrow a vision of hope.
Look well, therefore, to this Day.
Such is the salutation of the Dawn.

$\qquad\qquad\qquad\qquad\qquad$ — SANSKRIT

ARE YOU READY FOR SUCCESS?

What phase of success do you need to work on at this time in your life? Look at the list below, select the one/s that is relevant to you and write about it: Next draw a large circle on a sheet of paper, now create your own pie chart, showing your percentages.

1. Money . . . .

2. Power . . . .

3. Right Career Choice? . . . .

4. Relationships/work, family, significant other . . . .

5. Life Style . . . .

6. Being of Service to one's fellow man . . . .

7. Spiritual Values . . . .

Success is a journey, the journey you travel in life until you make your transition from the planet, you are forever creating and recreating a new you and new success.

To have success or to be successful in life, you must be willing to participate in your success and be successful (enjoy a larger experience of life and living). If you agree with this concept, and you want more aliveness in life sign your commitment below.

I . . . . am willing to participate in my success and I will do everything within my power to be actively involved in my program for success.

DAILY PROSPERITY MESSAGE

I am forever with the infinite Supply of God. It knows me,
claims me, and rushes to me.

I accept this Supply for myself and for everyone who is in need.

Prosperity is the law of my life. This law is continuously
operative in my affairs.

49

I now open my mind, body, purse, business, and all else in order that this prosperity may flow through me in abundant measure.

I am confident that I shall have plenty to meet every need when it is due.

My income is in the keeping of infinite wisdom.
My affairs are guided by Divine Intelligence.

All that the Father has is mine now.
Today I claim my good and today it is mine.

Prosperity flows through me in an uninterrupted stream, eliminating everything unlike itself.

There is nothing in me that can obstruct, congest, or retard my supply in any way.

My Supply is wherever I am. It comes to me from everywhere.

I accept my abundance, bounty, and opulence today.
I know that it is externalizing itself in my life and affairs.

I am not concerned about the limitations and fears of yesterday.
I know that right now everything is made rich.

I disclaim the idea that I am broke, despondent, poor, crushed, defeated, or dependent. New opportunities are now open to me.

Wherever I go, I shall meet prosperous people and prosperous conditions.

*I let blessings, money, and possessions flow to me
from every direction.*

*I believe that the law of Prosperity operating through me
will bless and enrich everyone I meet.*

I do not identify with lack, but practice the Presence of God.
– REVEREND, DR. DELIA SELLERS

Chapter 7

How to Survive in the Business World

The way to the top is much like a journey or a hunting trip. You may make many detours and it may seem at times that you have lost your way. Take heart, the detour may turn out to be missing information you need to complete your expedition.

Pay attention to your intuition and hunches along the way, for they will seldom lead you astray. Our mind is always working to help us realize our dream and desires. If you say to yourself, I need to learn to be more subtle, your mind will find a way to accommodate you. The mind is always working to help us achieve our desires. You may think to yourself, "I wouldn't want to work for a strict boss," Your mind hears, "strict boss," and it begins to look for ways to give you your desire. A year later you may find yourself working under an autocratic executive in a large corporation.

If you are an aggressive, cut-throat type of person, you will need to learn subtlety. The mind works to accommodate us, so it will provide an opportunity for you to learn how to be more subtle. However, learning a new skill is not easy. It may be very stressful for you, so you may decide to seek employment elsewhere; and that is okay. The road to the top of the corporate ladder is not always a straight one. What if you have to detour along the way? The valuable skills you develop will provide you a solid foundation. And the detour can act as a leverage to move you to the next rung of the ladder.Patience is an important trait you will need throughout your career. Patience with yourself and others.

Do not become wary, and disappointed with yourself if you are not moving as swiftly as you had envisioned. For you could be gathering valuable information that can assist you later in your climb up the corporate ladder.

As you move along your career path. Do a periodic assessment of your goals. Noting where you want to go and what steps you need to take to reach your objectives. Do this once a year, preferably at the beginning of the year.

Make this one of your New Year's resolutions. Sit down; take out a 8½ x 11 sheet of paper, turn it so the lines are vertical rather than horizontal and make 3 columns: Skills I possess, Skills I need to possess, Skills necessary for me to have to reach my desired goal. Be honest and truthful with yourself. If you feel you are too aggressive or passive, take an assertiveness class. Then you will have an objective assessment database from which to glean information.

Continue to look at ways you can improve your personal competence. See yourself as a piece of equipment. Are you an upgraded piece of equipment, or are you an outdated piece of equipment? Remember your employer is looking for value, not a warm body. Just, how valuable are you to the corporation? Have you taken a course lately to stay abreast of the newer technologies in your field? Can you be placed in more than one work environment within the corporation? Just how valuable are you? If you have limited skills, either professionally or personally you will soon be replaced. You will be replaced with a more skillful person.

How valuable you make yourself to the corporation determines how far you go up the corporate ladder. Even in companies where nepotism is practiced. If you show the corporation or top management how you can assist them in reaching their goals, a nitch will be created for you.

It is wise to have some basic knowledge about how corporations are structured and how they function. You need to know the rules to play the game.

All organizations are divided into two major structures: **Formal and Informal.**

The *formal structure* of a company is composed of all the official policies, rules, job titles, etc., that are designed to make the company work. The *informal structure* is composed of the friendship and association networks that unofficially make the organization function. For example, if you look for a job through the formal structure of an organization, you send a resume to the personnel manager. If you looking for a job through the informal structure of an organization, you call a friend in the organization who calls her/his buddy in the department of your choice, who talks to the boss, who calls you. Occasionally this can happen.

Every organization creates a formal structure which is intended to fulfill the goals of the organization. The formal structure is all the rules, policies, procedures, official job duties and division of labor created by the top management to fulfill organizational objectives. The ultimate purpose of every formal structure is to provide quality service or product and therefore, make money.

Formal Power and Influence: Businesses are generally divided into two divisions of labor, the staff and line. The staff (or support functions) usually includes all administrative positions: Examples are personnel, purchasing, accounting (payables and receivables) and training. Line personnel handle jobs which are directly involved with income production for the company. In a retail organization, line personnel include sales people and store managers. In hospitals, they are doctors and nurses. In manufacturing organizations, line personnel include factory workers and engineers or product designers.

Chain of Command and Protocol: According to Natasha Josefowitz, 1980, there are basically three levels of power in the chain of command continuum; *dependent power, intermediate power, and influence power.* People at the lowest rung on the ladder have *dependent power*. They have entry-level jobs which provide them with little control over their work situation. Also, they have little or no decision-making responsibility and a very narrow range of duties.

People with *intermediate power* have some decision-making responsibility and influence over others; but they are under the influence of higher-ups. Supervisors, managers, and senior professional staff are examples of middle-level positions.

Influence power, these positions are at the top of the chain of command. Examples of people with influence power are the President, Vice President, the Director, the Dean of the College, and the Hospital Administrator. The decisions these people make have the broadest impact on the organization.

Now that you have a working knowledge about the overall structure of an organization, remember that you are a key member; what you do can impact your career as you move up the corporate ladder.

You are an asset to the corporation. To get promoted, you need tangible and marketable skills that will assist the corporation in expanding.

Skills you will need to survive in the corporate world are:
1. Speaking skills
2. Presentation skills
3. Positive self-esteem
4. Desire for challenge
5. Creativity
6. Desire for power
7. Negotiation skills
8. Ability to delegate
9. Independence
10. Ability to Balance Empathy and Objectivity
11. Desire for change
12. Desire for competition
13. Opportunism
14. Wisdom

Speaking skills – You will need to have mastery over your ability to express your ideas and opinions in a logical, orderly manner. You will need to be able to think quickly, and speak to the issue when called upon, at a moments notice. A cost effective simplistic training program is a toastmistress or toastmaster group. For the club listing in your locality, check the phone directory or contact your local Chamber of Commerce.

Presentation skills – This is a three-fold process. We present ourselves through the way we speak, dress and interact with other people. It would be a good idea for you to attend one of the free wardrobe shows given by one of the local department stores. Call to ask when and if such event is being offered. If you are unable to attend a free session, it would be worth your money to have a color analysis done by a professional, to ascertain which colors best bring out your skin tone coloring. What is your body-type frame, and the best style clothing to wear to emphasize or de-emphasize certain body proportions?

If you wish to be successful, it is worth your time to give the right impression. What you choose to wear says something about how you wish to be seen. Your attire does not need to be expensive. It needs to be clean, neat, simple, and in good taste. Avoid wearing clothes that make you stand out. Let people notice you and your talents rather than your clothing. A suit or dress with jacket is always in good taste. It is wise to have a gray or blue suit in your wardrobe, additionally for females a beige, black or white dress. For men, black shoes are always in style. Women may want to have a pair of beige and navy blue shoes in their possession.

Everything you say is judged on two levels: *What you say and the way you deliver it.* Many people put themselves down by the words they use. The use of qualifying statements before you speak diminishes the impact of your message and also affects the impression others will have of you. Examples of this are: starting a sentence with, "May I say something," does not encourage people to listen. Other

sentence prefaces are "I don't know," "Maybe I should," "I kind of."
Examples of the use of superlatives are "terrific," "fantastic," "great,"
all detract from your presence.

It would help you to secure the services of a voice or theatrical
coach who has access to video feedback so you can see and hear how
you come across to others as you present yourself. Again in many
toastmasters club, this is sometimes available for free, but the feedback may not be as detailed as you might like.

If finances are a consideration for you. You can tape record a message play it back, to critique yourself. Also you can give a presentation standing in front of the mirror. Pay close attention to your body
posture, i.e. the way you hold your head to one side, raise one shoul-
der, body rigidity and breathing pattern.

Ask several friends or two different neighbors to critique your
presentation, and to give you objective feedback. Tell them you want
the truth, even if it is unpleasant. You might write out a list of things
you want them to check-off, to make it easier for them in their critique of you. Some people have trouble saying unpleasant things—
when asked for an opinion.

Positive Self-Esteem – I cannot say enough about positive self-
esteem. You will either fail or go to great heights in your career,
depending upon your measure of a positive self-image. A positive
self-image lays the foundation for our positive self-esteem. Our self-
esteem is the foundation for self-mastery. Self-mastery is a life long
process, for it is an accumulation of all the thoughts we have held
over the years of our life. The words we speak to ourselves and others are expressions of our thoughts and beliefs. So, to have self-mastery we must look at what we think about most of the time and what
we believe.

Who you are today is an accumulation of what you have, told
yourself and the beliefs you have formed as a result of your inner dia-
logue. We shape our life by the choices we make, which are influ-

enced by the thoughts we accept, or reject. *"For by thy words thou shalt be justified, and by thy words thou shalt be condemned," –* MATTHEW 12:37.

If you have a good opinion of yourself it can be eroded by having negative people around you. We influence and are influenced by the people with whom we associate. The key is a high self-esteem level. It is wise to take a refresher course to keep your level of self-esteem high. Read other books by the author: *Soft Power Negotiation Skills™*, *Light the Fire Within You*, *How To Improve Self-Esteem In The African American Child*, *Self-Esteem The Essence of You*, and *How To be A Success In Business*. In the back of this book is an audio cassette tape album you can order to help you maintain your positive self-esteem.

Mental imagery and visualization can be used, to help you create the job position you desire. To do this, find a quiet spot in your home. Turn off the radio and TV.; put on loose, comfortable clothing. Sit, take in a couple of deep breaths, then exhale slowly, and repeat the process again. Imagine yourself being in a calm peaceful and relaxing place, then bring to mind the job position you desire. See, in your imagination the location, (street, building, floor) be as specific as you can with the details. See yourself at your desk. Visualize the dress or suit you will be wearing and the title on your desk. Be sure to visualize your interview with your future boss. See him welcoming you and introducing you to the people who will be working for you. Visualize the salary you desire, flashing the figures across your mind's eye in bold, bright green colors. Money is green, so see lots of fresh green dollar bills. Do this exercise once a day. Just before you go to bed for 30 days, then once a week for 30 days. Repeat this process until you get the job position you desire.

Remember to sell yourself at every available opportunity. Your boss needs to know about the great things you have done, or are doing. However, be discreet and use tact. Right timing is very important when you are selling another person on yourself. The purpose of this exercise is to allow your imagination to brainstorm your environmental preferences. For a moment, allow yourself to create the perfect work environment for you.

Creative Visualization

Describe your environment (structure, office, outdoors/indoors, colors used, type of decor, furniture, location, etc.)

. . . .
. . . .
. . . .

How would you be dressed?

. . . .
. . . .
. . . .

How many people will you be working with, and how does your work interface with theirs?

. . . .
. . . .
. . . .

Where do you fit into the work hierarchy?

. . . .
. . . .
. . . .

What attitudes are encouraged and rewarded?

. . . .
. . . .
. . . .

What strengths will you be bringing with you?

. . . .
. . . .
. . . .

What would you be saying to yourself about your new career?

. . . .

. . . .

. . . .

Desire for challenge – You will need a compelling reason or reasons to inspire you onward with your career. Therefore, write out your goals. Keep them in view, so that you can see them often. What is your challenge? Is it to move to a better neighborhood? Get new braces for your child's teeth? Install a swimming pool or a Jacuzzi in your back yard? Get a weekly pedicure, manicure and facial? Make $50,000 a year? Become the first female corporate executive in your firm? For a man, it may be an additional $100,000 to pay for college expenses. You need a desire for challenge. A burning desire to achieve that will inspire you to want to move up the corporate ladder. If you have not given this much thought, take the time now to decide what you want in life.

What challenge or challenges would you like to overcome? Give yourself a time frame (one year, two years etc.). When do you plan to accomplish your goal? Remember to set realistic goals. You may need to enroll in adult education classes, attend jr. college or a university to acquire the necessary skills, for the job you desire. Maybe you will be the first person in your family to graduate from college. Do you have a strong enough reason, that will propel you, to move up the corporate ladder?

Creativity – I define creativity as risk taking behavior, without fear, utilizing problem solving skills. You will need to be very creative to know when to make the right moves that will move you forward on your career path.

Risk taking behaviors require that you use every bit of your ingenuity and creativity. It requires determination and effort. **Here are some of the areas you may encounter:**

1. Male dominated company that uses "old boy standards" to move up in the corporation. You are a female; you are stuck at a certain level and can't seem to get promoted. Do you file a grievance with the labor relations department? Do you file a grievance with the Equal Employment Opportunity Commission, or do you try to get a good evaluation and seek employment at a more progressive firm? How you respond will have a lot to do with your goals. Are you a female trying to change company policies of discrimination towards females? If your goal is to move ahead as swift as possible, you may not want to make waves. Even if you transfer out of the corporation, how do you know if you will receive a favorable recommendation? You may be given a formal letter of recommendation to take with you, and have an unfavorable phone call precede you. You will need to use your creative abilities to ascertain what course of action to take.

2. Do you know the rules of your corporation? *What are the office politics?* Do you have to play politics to move up in the corporation? What have others before you done to get promoted? Are there cliques in the organization? Do you need to be a part of one? If so, which one leads to advancement? How have other females advanced in the corporation? Is it necessary to have a non-business relationship with the boss to get promoted? It is wise to learn early what the formal and informal rules of the corporation are. Until you do, it is better to maintain detachment from all groups, until you know which is the "in group" (movers) and which is the "out group" (the watchers and gossiper). You may not want to become bosom buddies with the gossiper but you might want to listen in, to find out about the office politics and in-house happenings.

3. *Luncheon, business meeting, social engagement; you are new on the job!* You are invited by your boss to all of the above. Should

you accept all three invitations or decline all three. Until you know the rules of the corporation, you are safer attending a business meeting where the matters to be discussed will follow corporate protocol and thereby dictate how you and others will interact. Always keep before you your goals, you are there to move up the corporate ladder, not seek a husband or wife. If to seek a lover or mate is one of your goals, it is a good business practice to keep the two separate. It reduces the risk of emotional abuse for both parties.

4. *Help the boss look good* – Remember your first loyalty is to the corporation. Your goal is to help the corporation profit. If you present professional, ethical demeanor, you will be perceived that way and treated in that manner. However, as a female if you are at a social function and the boss makes an off-colored remark to you, you may have to take a risk, by telling him you are offended by the remark. The same applies for a male with a female boss. It is better to be able to look yourself in the mirror than to have your boss assume you like to be treated with disrespect.

Right timing is the key here. If your boss was inebriated when he/she made the remark, you might want to wait, when he/she is sober speak with him/her.

Let them know that you respect them, but you felt disrespect by the comment/s made by him/her. Say you like to treat others with respect and you like for others to treat you with respect.

Whenever you are in a *social gathering* and someone makes a *disrespectful comment to you, do not* join in the laughter, move away quickly to show your disapproval.

Whenever you engage in risk taking behavior without fear, it shows that you know how to use power and that you are not afraid of it.

Desire for power – To move up the corporate ladder you will need to have a healthy desire for power. *Power is the ability to get people to do what you want them to do, and the ability to avoid being forced to do what you don't want to do.* Some key guidelines to know about power are:

1. **Build relationships** – gratitude and obligation can give you power leverage. Make sure the people working under you have a positive impression of you. They are more likely to trust you and want to do as you suggest.

   Regardless of your position within an organization, you need to be aware of protocol. *Bosses generally want to know who's doing what, when, and with whom.* They never want to find out information through a second source. The key is to always keep your boss informed of your activities. Periodically update your superior; this gives you an opportunity to share some of the good things you are doing, make a request, or get feedback about your opportunities for advancement.

2. Your power base increases as the number of people dependent on you increases. How many people need your knowledge or input?

3. **Establish credibility** – stand behind what you say and do. Keep your word and follow through on your promises.

4. **Become an expert** – Develop a reputation as an expert, this way others will come to rely on you and defer to your judgment.

5. **Data control** – Control as much as possible the flow of information. To have privileged information that others desire can increase your power base immensely.

6. **Personal Control** – What resources are you able to control? The major ones are money, employees, equipment etc.

7. **Be interested in other people** – know how people feel about important issues; seek to win their respect.

8. **Know the sources of power** – Observe and listen in to the grapevine. Who are the movers in the organization? Who is quoted most often? Pay attention to these tidbits of information.

    Observe what gets rewarded and what receives disapproval. Notice what happens if deadlines are not met or procedures are not followed? If possible, try to find out why the boss seems to dislike someone or why someone was let go. All of this is valuable information that can aid you in your climb to the top of the corporation. Observe symbols of power and who has them: Symbols of power are any visible benefits which are offered to employees above a certain level example, company cars, choice parking spots, an office facing the ocean etc. Often these benefits are given to an employee who is on the way up the corporate ladder.

9. **Be willing to take a risk** – Be willing to risk the power you have to obtain more. There are no hard rules to follow, as when to take a risk, and when not to. But if you rely on your intuition, you will seldom go wrong. Remember, if you get fired it is not the end of the world. Sometimes you need to let go of something, to discover what you don't want.

10. **Avoid losing power** – Sidestep activities and projects that could have an adverse effect on the power you have.

11. **Be ethical** – Don't lie, cheat or break your promise.

12. **How to use power positively to impact the lives of others** – If you are in charge of memos, meetings agendas or schedules, others will need your approval. This will place you in a position of power.

13. **Be aware of how your actions are viewed by others** – Are you seen as supporting others, or do you have a label as a self-serving individual?

14. **Employees** – The greater your responsibilities, the more you need to rely on the cooperation and help of others. Unless the people working under you are loyal, they may not follow your orders. Seek to establish a trusting and bonding alliances of a few key people to leverage your power base?

    Remember, power is about forming and maintaining dependent and interdependent relationships with persons under your leadership. It can be good or bad, constructive or destructive. The choice is yours.

For whoever becomes great must render great service. Likewise, whoever finds themselves at the top must lose themselves at the bottom. Meaning you will need to trade your old self-image for a newer self-image that matches your title.

Also, everyone who is now at the top was once at the bottom. They had to create success for themselves and learn to accept their success image.

Your ability to negotiate and use power wisely will critically influence the outcome of your success. The use of Soft Power™ negotiation skills, will enable you to negotiate with others to get what you want, and still have harmonious relations with them.

All successful people in positions of authority know how to negotiate, and their negotiation skills are an asset to them and the organization they serve. These are the factors involved in effective negotiation skills.

Negotiation Skills
Factors involved in negotiation are:

1. **Communication** – Listen and act on what we hear. To send and receive information with understanding.

2. **Relationship** – Personal/Impersonal. You will need to maintain a degree of detachment whether you are dealing with a friend, family member, or business associate.

3. **Attitude** – Positive/Negative. Others tend to mirror our attitude and behavior. Be positive in outlook if you want a positive outcome.

3. **Self-Image** – Self-Worth, deserving. Project the image you want and deserve to have your needs met.

4. **Self-Esteem** – Right to have one's basic needs met; to esteem and accept oneself as valuable.

5. **Life Position** – Powerful/powerless; choice/no choice; independent/dependent; control/no control.

6. **Self-Confidence** – Courage to ask for what you want, expecting to get it; belief in oneself.

7. **Creativity** – Ability to use your ingenuity in problem solving situation.

8. **Orientation to Life** – Personality style/conflict resolution style. The way you interact with others is indicative of your learned coping patterns to handle frustration, conflict, anger, and criticism.

Negotiation is a process which occurs any time we attempt to influence the behavior of another so as to cause them to comply with our wishes and desires. It implies that a desire demands satisfaction and a need is unfulfilled.

Ability to delegate – The ability to delegate is a skill worth developing in yourself. As you move up the corporate ladder and assume more responsibilities, you will need the assistance of others to maximize your time, effort and resources.

Foremost of all, *decide what tasks you will delegate and which you will do yourself.* Once you delegate, let the individuals know up front that you may need to make corrections as you go along and that you will need input from them; also tell them that you will need to have periodic reviews to gauge the success of the project/tasks. This way they will be expecting to be accountable to you for their work activities. If you lay out the ground rules before hand, they are less likely to view you as meddling when you inquire about their activities later. You might want to agree on an acceptable review conference schedule. If the project before you has a time deadline, you may need to have a weekly or monthly review.

Here are some points to keep in mind as you decide what to delegate to whom:

1. **The buck stops with you.** You will be held accountable whether the project fails or succeed. You will lose the loyalty of your subordinates if they are blamed for the failure. Also your superiors will not respect you if you place the blame on your subordinates. Just admit that the situation did not turn out as you expected.

2. **Know what to delegate.** If you have been asked to handle the task, don't delegate it. They want your expertise. Even though the task may be very simple. Someone respects your abilities. Be glad.

3. **Be selective.** Delegate the right task to the right person. Try to match the skills of the task to the person. You will be less likely to hear complaints and you will be pleased to know that the job is in competent hands.

4. **Be explicit.** Make certain your delegates understand what they are to do. Have well defined goals. Ask for clarification and feedback. If they can state back to you the overall concept of what you said you have obtained your objective.

5. **Responsibility.** Try to foster a sense of responsibility in your delegates. Let them know you are counting on them to do well.

6. **Authority.** Define the limits of authority they will have. Let them know that the authority may be shared between you and them. However, if at all possible assign them total responsibility for minor job tasks. Let them know that they need to check with you if ever they are doubtful about overstepping their boundaries.

7. **Decision-making.** Plan on making the big decisions yourself and let them analyze, advise and recommend.

8. **Independent action.** Encourage independence. Allow your delegates to act, without checking with you before their every move. This will help them feel that you have confidence in them. Also it will help them to feel more competent in what they are doing. Focus more on "what" they do, rather than "how" they carry out your instructions.

9. **Expect excellence.** Set the example, expect high standards of workmanship from both yourself and those working under you. Let them know in advance that you want quality workmanship.

Think of ways you can reinforce this behavior through some form of positive reinforcement.

10. **Rewards.** People will not work for long without some form of reward. Be supportive. Try to operate more as a team leader. Encourage and coach rather than dictate. Encourage them to succeed. Let them and others above you, know when they have done a good job. This will bolster their morale, and motivate them to work harder to be a good team member.

Know when things have run off track. Make necessary corrections when needed. If negative feedback is needed use the sandwich approach. State two positive factors, give the negative corrective feedback, then end with a positive statement. Let them know they are still an important part of the team. Take every opportunity to build up their morale and they will in turn do the same for you.

11. **Build trust and respect.** Strive for mutual trust and respect from those working under your leadership. Take the necessary time to build an atmosphere of trust, respect, cooperation and open communication. This may take some time, but the long term benefits are worth it to you.

If this is your first time having subordinates work under you, be understanding. Don't place the whole work load on them at once. Share some of the work load. It will help them to see you as a caring superior. It will make them work even harder to support you and your goals. The ability to delegate is an art and will take time and practice. Be a good team manager. Working as a team manager allows you to demonstrate independent leadership.

12. **Independence** – To move up the corporate ladder you will need to show that you are a leader. Leaders do not need group

approval or reinforcement to bolster their self-esteem. They tend to view groups as a means of sharing ideas, information and problem solving.

All corporate executives have to be willing to take risks to advance their careers. Risk taking means to act, in hope, that the outcome is favorable. If you have a fear of failure or are uncertain, you may want to be more pragmatic and avoid taking big risks. *Confront your fears and act when you think it wise.* Rely on your intuition to guide you.

Always have a clear idea of how much power and authority you have. Know your limitations. Use wisdom and good judgment. There will be times when you should not act.

Rely on your intuitions to guide you.

Ability to Balance Empathy and Objectivity. – It is wiser to access any situation before you act. You want to take care that your objectivity is not hampered by your feelings. As a supervisor, you will need to play many roles; you need to be able to move in and out of a role quickly and gracefully. You can be empathetic to the needs of others and still maintain objectivity; the key is detachment. View yourself as a judge who is giving an impartial decision; this way you can maintain a healthy balance between empathy and objectivity. Know your limitations and be honest with yourself. There are times when you may need to side step a situation because your objectivity is clouded by personal experiences.

Desire for change. – Do not be fearful if you are fired. Being fired may be the best thing that could happen to your career. You may have reached a plateau in your former job. A variety of experiences can be critical to the advancement of your career.

The path to the top of the corporate ladder is not always straight. You may need to move horizontally or diagonally to advance your career. Move to another if it is to your advantage.

If you can get free training in high technology or computer training, take it. You may have to start on a lower entry pay level, but the ability to advance within the corporation may be excellent.

Be willing to take a risk. *Comfort is not always growth.* You may be very comfortable in your present job environment, but how far will you have advanced in ten years? Will you be making the $70,000 you had set out to make within 10 years if that is your goal? Always maintain a competitive edge for yourself.

Desire for competition. You will need a strong, healthy desire for competition to move up the corporate ladder. There may be times when the odds are against you. However, if you have a strong drive to achieve, you can overcome the tendency to become discouraged or wanting to quit. This is the time when a strong faith in a power greater than yourself can provide the courage to hang in there. A strong faith in God assures you that you are not alone. One of my favorite bible quotations to use as a "pick me up," is "Greater is He that is within you, than he that is in the world."

Be willing to take a risk to advance your career. Plan before hand to have a contingency plan in case things do not turn out as you had planned. Be willing to compromise or negotiate if necessary. Try to gauge in advance how far you can go before you reach a point of no return. *Know when to push and when to pull. Also know when to quit.* Don't be discouraged if you risk and lose. Nothing ventured—nothing gained. Most people who achieve greatness have failed. They were able to learn from their failure and became strategically better the second, or third time around.

Opportunism. – To succeed in Corporate America you will need to be an opportunistic entrepreneur. Each day you live, you tread on uncharted terrain. Keep a keen eye. Be forever looking out for new opportunities; when you see one, seize it. It may not come back again. Keep an open mind. Be kind, cordial and considerate to all people regardless of the sex, race or creed. The person you help may be the one to aid you after a devastating blow to your career. Pause often to count your gains and your losses. Whatever you do, do it with style and class. Do it with gusto, heart, vim and vigor. If you are a leader act like a leader. Remember, all good leaders know how to follow when necessary. Aim high, but know how to fall to grace.

The path to the top of the corporate ladder is often arduous, rugged, and stormy. Stop, often, along the way to smell the roses and enjoy the scenery on your way to the top.

As you move up the corporate world take the prayer of serenity with you.

The Serenity Prayer
God, Grant me the serenity to accept the things I cannot change,
The Courage To Change The Things I Can,
And The Wisdom To Know The Difference.

The Rugged Roads Of Life
Life is an ever increasing spiral,
on the path to human perfection.
It matters not the hue of your skin,
the color of your eyes, not the color of your hair.
For self-mastery is an inner process,
that happens each time you overcome an obstacle.
No one can ever determine,
the depth of your learning experience.
So continue on your journey, to overcome
your stiffest challenges,
For no one will ever know, the depths of your overcoming.
Continue to strive for excellence in every thing you do.
For the path to fulfillment and happiness
is the rugged road of life.
IDA GREENE

Do You Really Want Success?

We create our world through our thoughts about life in general and ourselves in particular. If you are clear in your thinking and affirmative in your mind, you will find self fulfillment because you will attract positive conditions, and positive constructive people, like yourself. Though we are not able to control the circumstances of our life; we are able to control our response to people, situations, circumstances and events through our beliefs. Anything you believe in an air of positive expectancy will happen. Therefore, if you desire success, wealth, abundance, and riches believe you will achieve it. Believe this with deep feeling, and you will experience it.

To have success or be successful, you must first create a success consciousness or mind set. Everything is created first from a thought pattern. All ideas, plans, purpose or desires are created in your thoughts first before they become a reality. Through the natural law of correspondence, we can change any undesirable conditions. It requires the ability to control your thoughts to correspond to the desired conditions and objectives you have set in your mind. The mind can only hold one thought at a time, lack or prosperity, scarcity or abundance, poverty or wealth, success or failure. You can choose to focus on prosperity, abundance, wealth, or success.

The best way to rid yourself of a negative belief about your self, money, success or your capability is to substitute the thought for a new thought. We can never dismiss a thought. A negative thought about money, lack, or limitation can be replaced with thoughts of abundance, and prosperity. To receive more good in your life, you must open your mind to accept a greater good. For you to receive more money, you must prepare your mind to expect more wealth, abundance, and prosperity.

The following is a mental treatment by Reverend Sheila Alberts of San Diego, CA to prepare your mind to accept a greater good. Write your name in the blank space.

74

This treatment is for (Your name)..
God is love. There is only one love, and you are aware of it. You are aware that you are wanted, needed, and loved. You belong to the universe. God has not rejected you, and no one else can. You do not reject yourself. There is no condemnation or judgment operating through you. Every plant that my heavenly father hath not planted is rooted up and cast out. This word establishes perfect circulation, assimilation, and elimination. Whatever there is that does not belong to you is eliminated.

(Your name).., you have a consciousness of belonging to life, of feeling the divine presence, and you now accept your good! You have a complete sense of being unburdened, and you enter into the joy of living, which is reflected in every aspect of your experience. You have faith in yourself! The perfect action of God cast out all unlike God, and I (Your name)...
give thanks that it is doing this right now for you ....

REVEREND SHEILA ALBERTS

We must be willing to take risks, to walk forth on our faith of a perfect outcome, even though our success may not be visible.

Risk

To laugh is to risk appearing a fool.
To weep is to risk appearing sentimental.
T reach out for another is to risk involvement.
To expose feelings is to risk exposing your true self.
To place your ideas, dreams, before a crowd is to risk their
  loss.
To love is to risk not being loved in return.
To live is to risk dying.
To hope is to risk despair.
To try is to risk failure.
But risks must be taken, because the greatest hazard in life

is to risk nothing.
The person who risks nothing, does nothing, has nothing,
and is nothing.
They may avoid suffering and sorrow but they cannot learn,
*   feel, change, grow, love, live.*
Chained by their certitudes, they are a slave, they have forfeit-
*   ed their freedom. Only a person who risks is free.*
                    – ANON

*   I choose to look at my assets instead on my liabilities.*
Nothing can interfere with the perfect right action of God
Almighty within me. I refuse to be governed by the past.
Circumstances have no power over me. I am opening the
way for right action to express in and through my life now.
*   I am one with my prosperity.*
            Excerpted from *All About Prosperity*
        by JACK AND CORNELIA ADDINGTON, DeVorss & Co.

Abundance

I identify myself with abundance.
The abundance of God fills my every good desire, right now.
I surrender all fear and doubt.
I let go of all uncertainty.
The Freedom of God is my freedom.
The Power of God is my power.
I know there is no confusion, no lack of confidence.
The Presence of God is with me.
The Mind of God is my mind.
            – GASTON GONZALEZ, Glendale CA

How To Cope With The Loneliness And Isolation of Success

Are you ready for success? If you were asked this question by an unsuspecting person more than likely your immediate response would be "yes". Then the words "Why do you ask?" would probably flash across your mind. Seldom, if ever will anyone ask you this question in your lifetime. Most of us are never questioned as to whether we are ready for success by anyone including ourselves. It is little wonder that we lack motivation and drive for our goals. How can we ever marshal forth our inner resources to act if we have never asked the question of ourselves? There are in fact many questions you will need to ask yourself before you embark on a journey of success. The first question to ask yourself is:

1. Do you want success? Remember success will mean different things to different people.

2. Write out your definition of success.

The answers you have just written will help you decide if you are ready for success.

3. Ask yourself if you have the skills to handle the task/project before you?

4. Do you need to acquire further training or education? Do you have a written plan of what you will do or how long it will take to get the skills required for your profession? Write it now.

5. What resources(materials/finances) do you need to accomplish your goals.

6. What plans do you have to generate the support you need, be it tactical or monetary?

7. Ask yourself' Do I have the discipline to stay focused on my dream project irrespective of obstacle or disappointment?

8. Now the dual question, is this something you want to do? Do you get excited each time you think about this project?

To Discover Your Inner Self, Ask Yourself These Questions
1. Who Am I?   I am:

2. Finish this Sentence:
   "I am a product of my upbringing because" :

3. What I Want From Life Is:

4. My Likes Are:

5   My Dislikes Are:

6. I Am Good At Doing:

7. Finish this statement, "If I could only do one kind of work in life, it would be:"

I Accept My Self, Health and Wealth

It is right, and just for me to have my needs met.
It is right and just for me to ask for and receive what I want.
I am accepting of others showing appreciation and love to me.
I am deserving of love, affection, right treatment, and respect.
    I am created in the image and likeness of God, it feels good.
I am created in the image of God, who is perfection of body,
    mind, and soul.

God cares for me and provides for all my needs.
I do not need to ask, my loving God already knows what I need.
I am proud to have a rich, royal, wise and spiritual lineage.
All of my needs are abundantly supplied. I now cease all worry
    and concern so that God can work through me.

I know I am loved beyond measure; God wants the best for me.
I give up all struggle as, I allow God to point the way.
I am patient with myself, and God as I evolve to my higher self.
I become a better person daily. I am worthy to be God's child.
I accept all of God's creation, starting with myself.
    – Adapted by IDA GREENE

Daily Guide to Happiness

PRAY: It is the greatest power on earth.

READ: It is the fountain of wisdom.

GIVE: It is too short a day to be stingy.

PLAY: It is the secret of perpetual youth.

SAVE: It is the secret of security.

WORK: It is the price of success.

LOVE: It is the road to happiness.

CARE: It is a God given privilege.

LAUGH: It is the music of the soul.

THINK: It is the source of power. – NORMAN VINCENT PEALE

Purpose, A Reason for Living

*Purpose gives meaning to life. Purpose gives Joy, and
Zest to living. What is your Desire, your Dream? When
our eye is on our goal, we are not so easily disturbed
by things around us.*

*Purpose awakens new trains of thoughts in our mind. Our pur-
pose directs these trains of thought into new fields of
achievement.*

*To succeed in life we must have some great purpose in mind;
some goal toward which we would like to achieve. Find a
purpose, today.*

– ANON

To Discover Your Mission In Life

1. Finish this statement, "I am the happiest when I:"

2. Finish this statement, "I am most unhappy:"

   a. When I am –

   b. When I have to –

   b. When I need to –

3. Finish this statement, "I am the happiest at work when I":

4. Finish this statement, "I am most unhappy at work:"

   a. When I am –

   b. When I have to –

   c. When I need to –

5.   My goals in the following areas are
:**Personal:**

    a.   One year goal –

    b.   Five year goal –

    c.   Ten year goal –

Professional

    a.   One year goal –

    b.   Five year goal –

    c.   Ten year goal –

Spiritual

    a.   One year goal –

    b.   Five year goal –

    c.   Ten year goal –

Social

    a.   One year goal –

b.   Five year goal –

c.   Ten year goal –

d.   What beliefs do you hold, that block your personal, professional, social, spiritual growth?

6.   My 1 year, 5, and 10 year goals in the following areas are: write a **month and year** when you plan to achieve **each goal**

Career Goals –

Future Goals –

Relationships –

Social Activities –

To Discover Your Passion, Ask Yourself These Questions:

1. What things in life give me the greatest pleasure and satisfaction? Write these down now. Select one area where you feel least fulfilled, write about this:

    Personal:

    Professional:

    Social:

    Spiritual:

2. What things do others praise or compliment you on? Do you agree with them? Are you currently doing this type of work? If your answer is "no", Why?

    List ways you can develop, in this area/these skills.

To Discover Your Strengths:

1. Name characteristics or traits you have that set you apart from others.

2. To find your weaknesses:
    List areas of your personality that you would like to improve.

3. To Enhance Your Self-Image, ask yourself, How do I see myself in relation to?

    a. Other persons with similar skills

    b. Create an image of what you would like to do, or become. Spend five minutes each day reflecting on the new person you will become.

Prayer Treatment For Right Employment

There is a place for me in the job market and I expect to find it. It is the right place, the position for which I am both qualified and ready. Within me as I speak is an intelligence that knows what is my right job/employment, where it is, and when I will find it. I now call upon this power to guide me in the right direction. I release all anxiety. I wait with confidence as I listen to the divine intuition which will show me the next step to take. I accept my right employment now. I am open minded and willing to be guided.
– Christ Church Unity Prayer Tower, San Diego, CA

85

How To Get What You Want In Life
You Can Have Anything You Want –
If You Want It Badly Enough.
You Can Be Anything You Want To Be,
Have, Anything You Set Out To Accomplish –
If You Will Hold To That Desire
With Singleness Of Purpose.
– ROBERT COLLIER

The Power Of Imaging Our Possibilities
Go confidently in the direction of your dreams.
Live the life you have imagined.
– HENRY DAVID THOREAU

African Proverb
The only constant in the universe is change.

Chapter 8

How to Cope With Despair, Defeat and Failure

Success is two ends of the same stick. Whether you fail or succeed will be determined by your perception of whatever it is you want to achieve.

One of the afflictions that plaque human being the most is the tendency to hold on to disappointment, defeat, feelings of despair, and failure beyond its therapeutic point. When this happens energy accumulates in the body, and manifests as tension (stress) which is easily eliminated through activity or negative energy build up without release which I call stress. Not all stress is negative or bad for us.

Stress is a natural and normal part of life. It is a result of your interaction with your environment. Stress when utilized, I refer to as dynamic tension. This form of stress is built up as a result of our energy, motivation, and excitement. And when it is discharged creates a momentum that is a natural high. I refer to this process as good stress or Eustress. On the other hand stress that causes us to have migraine headaches, high blood pressure, or ulcers is a negative, and debilitating form of stress that works against us feeling balanced or peaceful inside our body. Much of the stress we experience results from emotional tension and confictual relationships. It seems as if we like to suffer, and be miserable. We complain about how rotten life is. We are goal seeking, goal striving individuals by nature.

We take the chaos in our lives, and turn it into order and balance. When our energy is negatively used we feel stressed, and out of sorts. This results sometimes because we have learned ineffective ways to solve the day to day problems we encounter. The result is a learned pattern of poor coping. Sometimes the solution to our problems is to

Let Go, and Let God take over our problems, and worries. We are such "fix it people" that we rarely seek help from other people, let alone God. Instead we continuously think about our problems, concerns, and worries; wondering when and how the right outcome will occur. We need to let go to release stressful energy from our body.

To be successful in any endeavor, it will require you to have energy, vim and vigor. This vim and vigor can not be bought in a bottle, taken in a pill, or ingested in a chemical or substance. Whenever we go against the natural law of our body's chemical mechanism, we cause congestion, and blockage of the body's hormonal neurotransmitter process. This hormone reaction takes place in the sympathetic and parasympathetic nervous system. It was first described by Dr. Hans Selye as stress.

In the words of Dr. Hans Selye, the father of stress research, "Life is no longer an episode." When the body experiences a stress reaction, it halts the body's natural hormonal process. Once a stress response occurs, it blocks the natural sequence of hormone elimination through physical activity and prevents the body from performing as it was originally designed to function. Modern life does not offer us the luxury to jog for twenty minutes every time we find ourselves angry or upset.

Few people are aware of how often they activate their body's stress response on a day-to-day basis. Even fewer are consciously aware of the specific events they do repeatedly that causes them to be stressed. The end result and major problem is an accumulation of stress hormones within the body brought on by a world that has become too busy, too crowded, and too complex.

Not every stress event we encounter will cause a stress response within our body. Our hormonal stress response is an archaic bodily response, and unless you need to be physical, it is an inappropriate response for the life stressors we encounter today such as: elevators, long lines, burnt toast etc. Many of our stress responses are triggered by events that have no physical solutions. The culprit is usually your personality style and poor coping skills. As we pass through life, we collect bad habits. We need to sort out our bad habit from the good and seek to reinforce the good ones.

At the end of each day, ask yourself, how many times did I activate my sympathetic nervous system today? And, to the best of your recollection, attempt to recall the specifics of the incident that caused you to feel a negative emotion. The goal is to reduce your production of stress hormones. This can be summed up in one word-COPING. Coping is a skill not unlike typing. If you want to type 75 words per minute-you have to work at it a little bit every day. If you want to handle adversity without getting upset or angry, you will need to work at it everyday. Better coping skills can be the habit that you use to replace the stress response.

Symptoms of Stress

Symptoms of stress can be categorized as physical symptoms, behavioral symptoms, or emotional symptoms. After looking over the symptoms, think about this past month. How many times have you experienced each of these symptoms? e.g. Once, twice, three times, and so on. Physical symptoms of headache, stomach ache, backache, muscle tension, diarrhea, heartburn, constipation, grinding teeth, skin rash, or a frequent need to urinate.

Beside our physical symptoms, you may experience other behavioral symptoms like blaming others, telling untruths, bossiness, irritability, impatience, anger inflexibility, drinking, taking aspirin or pain relievers, and difficulty meeting commitments.

Emotional symptoms include nervousness, anxiety, worry, fatigue, depression, fearfulness, hopelessness, difficulty concentrating, forgetting important things, crying easily, and not being able to turn off certain thoughts.

Managing Stress: Stress and Cortisol

Your body's chemistry is altered by how you interpret events. Negative interpretations elevate cortisol levels which suppresses the immune system, increases cholesterol, disturbs digestion, causes imprinting and insomnia.

Exercise is the most beneficial tool to eliminate the stress response and to provide a state of wholeness, and wellness. Exercise is the key, and its duration is vital. You must sustain your exercise period for a minimum of 20 minutes. Learn to modulate your intensity or pace until you can last for the prescribed duration. The prescribed level is frequently derived from the following equation: 80% of (220 minus your age) = maximum target heartbeat. Exercise a minimum of three-times per week to derive the benefits. Pick a Monday, Wednesday, Friday, or make it a family affair on Saturday. Its what works best.

Another stress elimination technique is the *Relaxation Response*. This is a conscious discipline that when practiced regularly alleviates the symptoms of stress. The directions are uncomplicated and with minimal effort can be accomplished be nearly everyone. Select a quiet uninterrupted place. Assume a comfortable sitting position, close your eyes, and let your body go limp by relaxing all of your muscles. Push all the busy thoughts out, and quiet your mind. Pay attention to your breathing and as you exhale, repeat to yourself the number ONE. The bottom line is, we can win against stress by being aware and taking the necessary action. An awareness of stress hormones and their accumulation is essential. The action steps are for us to work at decreasing our production of stress hormones and be proactive in its elimination.

There is a difference between complacency and satisfaction. If you are complacent, you are lying down on the job, but if you give satisfaction to God, yourself and others, you enjoy a greater fullness of life. And fulfillment brings satisfaction.

How to Program Your Mind for Success

The way we think and feel about ourselves is critical to how much energy, aliveness, and joy we experience daily. If our mental state is preoccupied with worry, doubt, anger, hate, or negative, warped thinking, we are likely to experience both physical and mental fatigue. When we hate ourselves, disrespect ourselves, hold ourselves in contempt, have low self-worth, or low self-esteem, it affects our total being. To be successful in anything, daily you need energy, aliveness, enthusiasm, and joy.

Are you ready for success? If you were asked this question by an unsuspecting person more than likely your immediate reply would be a resounding "yes." Then the words," why do you ask?" would probably flash across your mind or flow from your lips. Seldom, if ever will anyone ask you this question in your lifetime. Most of us are never questioned as to whether, we are ready for success by anyone, including ourselves. It is little wonder that we lack motivation and drive for our goals. How can we ever marshal forth our inner resources to act if we have never asked the question of ourselves? There are many questions you will need to ask of yourself before you embark on your journey of success. The first question to ask yourself is:

1. Do you want success? Remember success will means different things to different people.

2. Write your definition of success.

The answers you have just written will help you decide if you are ready for success.

3. Ask yourself if you have the skills to handle the task/project before you?

4. Do you need to acquire further training or education? Do you have a written plan of what you will do or how long it will take to get the skills required for your profession? Write a mini business plan now.

   a. Mission statement- Your mission statement should be one that can be understood by a twelve year old child and recited by you without a moment's hesitation.

   b. Your goals and objectives –

   c. Your plan to accomplish your objectives –

   d. Your marketing plan and strategy –

5. What resources (material/finances) do you need to accomplish your goal/s.

6. What plans do you have to generate the support you need be it tactical or monetary.

7. Next ask yourself, "do I have the discipline to stay focused on

my dream project irrespective of obstacle or disappointment?"

8. Now the dual question, Is this something you want to do?

9. Do you get excited each time you think about this project?

It takes courage to live in the face of adversity, or when all around you is in total chaos and your world seems to be falling apart. Discouragement is a luxury you can not afford. You need to have enough faith to believe in God's promise to you "that HE will never leave you alone nor abandon you." This brings to mind a poem by James Dillet Freeman entitled, "I am There."

I Am There

Do you need me? I am there.
You cannot see Me, yet I am the light you see by.
You cannot hear Me, yet I speak through your voice.
You cannot feel Me, yet I am the power at work in your hands.
I am at work, though you do not understand My ways.
I am at work, though you do not recognize My works.
I am not strange visions. I am not mysteries.
Only in absolute stillness, beyond self, can you know Me
*   as I am, and then but as a feeling and a faith.*
Yet I am there. Yet I hear. Yet I answer.

When you need Me, I am there.
Even if you deny Me, I am there.
Even when you feel most alone, I am there.
Even in your fears, I am there.
Even in your pain, I am there.

I am there when you pray and when you do not pray.
I am in you and you are in Me.

Only in your mind can you feel separate from Me, for only in
your mind are the mists of "yours" and "mine."
Yet only with your mind can you know Me and experience Me.

Empty your heart of empty fears.
When you get yourself out of the way I am there.
You can of yourself do nothing, but I can do all.
And I am in all.

Though you may not see the good, good is there, for I am there.
I am there because I have to be, because I am.
Only in Me does the world have meaning; only out of Me does
the world go forward.
I am the law on which the movement of the stars and the
growth of living cells are founded.
I am the love that is the law's fulfilling.
I am assurance.
I am peace.
I am oneness.
I am the law that you can live by.
I am the love that you can cling to.
I am your assurance.
I am your peace.
I am one with you.
I Am.
Though you fail to find Me, I do not fail you.
Though your faith in Me is unsure, My faith in you never
wavers, because I know you, because I love you.
Beloved, I am there.
— JAMES DILLET FREEMAN

Fifteen Tips on How to Get Ahead

1. Accept yourself. Stop being your own worst critic. Stand in front of a mirror, pat yourself on the back and congratulate yourself for the good things you did today. Be your own best friend.

2. Seize your dreams. List your 10 most cherished dreams, and do one thing today to help make the first one a reality. Do something tomorrow towards realizing the second and continue down the list.

3. Seize the year. Tell yourself this year is going to be your year. Write down 10 things you will accomplish in the new year and place the list where you will see it every day.

4. Seize the day. Write down each morning, in priority order, 10 things you will accomplish today. Starting at the top, check off each task as it is completed.

5. Take control of your career. Ask yourself, Dennis Kimbro says, what job or career would give you so much personal satisfaction that you would do it for free. Make a move right now- check the help wanted ad or fill out an employment or college application- to help bring about heart's desire.

6. Make a personal budget, and start saving at least 10 percent of your monthly earnings.

7. Improve your love life if you are married or otherwise attached. Re-evaluate the relationship. Is it missing something? Is there something you're not getting from it? Or something you're not giving to it? Identify the problem and the opportunity for change. Then discuss with your partner what's needed and commit to make the change today.

To Improve your love life if you are single and looking for Ms. Right or Mr. Right. Make a game plan. Re-evaluate yourself first. Look for ways to accentuate your attractiveness. Circulate in groups where you would most likely find the man or woman of your dreams. And when you find him or her, swallow your pride, overcome your shyness and ask for a date. If you ask, you will lose sometimes. If you don't ask, you will lose all of the time.

8. Improve your mind. Turn off the TV and pick up a book. Attend a lecture or an interesting play. Enroll in a class or classes at a local college or business school.

9. Improve your body – Part I. After consulting your doctor, create a personal exercise routine. Exercise your exercise plan by walking, jogging, swimming or bicycling.

10 Improve your body – Part II. Adopt a nutritious diet plan and stick to it. Seek professional help, if necessary.

11. Improve your appearance. Get a new hairdo, dress or suit. Treat yourself to a relaxing body massage or a few minutes in a hot sauna.

12. Work on your interpersonal relationships. Open up the lines of communication with co-workers, friends and loved ones. If an old insult or misunderstanding is complication your life, resolve to resolve the conflict with the person involved. Drop it, talk it out or get out of the relationship.

13. Avoid negative people and negative thoughts. It's in your best interest to get rid of negative "friends." You don't need people in your life who make you feel bad by putting you down. And self-talk like "I cannot, I should not, I must not" keep you from

getting what you want. Negative thoughts can make you sick.

14. Renew and deepen your spiritual faith. Meditate on the mysteries and wonder of life. Commit yourself and have faith in something bigger than your personal striving.

15. Stop procrastinating. Re-read numbers 1 through 14 above. Make a commitment to follow through. Regularly review your progress throughout the year. Do it today. Do it now!

If You Have a Problem

If you have a problem that bothers you inside and time does little to assure you that it will subside. Then draw upon your inner strength and formulate a plan; and of time you think you can't remember that you can listen to your deepest voice where reason still remains and take control of your own life to minimize the strain. Strip away the fantasy, the negatives, the doubts, the anger, the hostility and guilt recurrent bout. Try to shift into a course that is positive in tone to communicate your feelings so that you are not alone. A pattern of improvement in the change that you'll be winning. If you'll just let a single step become a new beginning.
— BRUCE B. WILMER

Affirmations

Affirmations are short statements that, when repeated in a consistent manner, promote coping. When confronted by an unexpected event, use the affirmation "I can handle it," while breathing in. When experiencing moments of anxiety, anger or tenseness, use the affirmation "I am relaxed." Think "I am" while breathing in and "relaxed" while breathing out.

97

If you are a spiritual person, recite bible quotations such as the ones below to release stress build up or tension from your body.

He will take care of his flock like a shepherd; he will gather the lambs together and carry them in his arms; he will gently lead their mothers. – CHRONICLES 40:11

Watch for the new thing I am going to do. It is already happening, you can see it now. – CHRONICLES 43:19

Cast Your Burden On The Lord, And He Will Sustain You. – PSALM 55:22

Affirm:
Today I refuse to worry about old wrongs.
Yesterday ended at midnight.
         – DOLLY SEWELL, NOTTINGHAM, ENGLAND

Say to yourself:

I express God today, and I am filled with the joy of living. Every task I perform carries with it its own measure of satisfaction. I am always doing something that needs to be done, and when I fill this need, whether it is mine or someone else, I am creating satisfaction. Satisfaction is the state of my consciousness today. My every thought focuses on abundant supply. Therefore my every need is filled, and my every desire is gratified. There is order in the arrangement of my affairs, now and always. I think on divine order, and divine order is manifested in all areas of my life and affairs.

I give thanks that the kingdom of heaven is within me, and that I have come to know, the eternal presence. Any incompleteness or shortcomings of my past are forgotten. There is only my consciousness of what I am and have today. My peace is the foundation of the inner work I have accomplished, and the trials I have surmounted. It

*is the handiwork of God working through me that gives me complete
satisfaction. As I make this divine connection each day I dwell in the
house of the God.*

Letting Go

LETTING GO *does not mean to stop caring-it means not to take
responsibility for someone else.*

LETTING GO *is no to enable others-it's to allow learning from
natural consequences.*

LETTING GO *is to admit your own powerlessness, which means
the outcome is not in your hands.*

LETTING GO *is not to try to change or blame others-but to make
the most of yourself.*

LETTING GO *is not to care for-but to care about.*

LETTING GO *is not to fix-but to be supportive.*

LETTING GO *is not to be in the middle arranging-but to be on the
sidelines, cheering.*

LETTING GO *is not to be protective-it's to permit another to face
reality.*

LETTING GO *is not to deny-but to accept.*

LETTING GO *is not to nag, scold or argue-it is to search out my
own shortcomings and correct them.*

LETTING GO *is not to adjust everything to your desires-but to take
each day as it comes, and cherish yourself in it.*

LETTING GO *is not to criticize and regulate others-but to grow
and live for the future.*

LETTING GO *is to fear less, and love more.*

— ANON

IT'S A SPECIAL DAY

*Something is occurring, something new is stirring. Something
the of the Spirit, blesses me today. Energies are swarming,
totally transforming. Something of the Spirit blesses me with
light.*

99

Knowledge is provided, I am being guided. Something of the Spirit blesses me with light. I have perfect leading to the good I'm needing. Something of the Spirit blesses me with light.

I accept my blessing; through it I'm expressing something of the Spirit Gloriously good. Every trouble ceases; all my joy increases. Something of the Spirit blesses me with good.

It's a special day, Its a special day. I can feel it deeply in a special way. It's a special day, it's a special day. I can feel it deeply in a special way.

— WARREN MEYER, GEORGE A. MINOR

Chapter 9

DEVELOP YOUR SELF-ESTEEM TO ACHIEVE SUCCESS

SELF ESTEEM: ARE YOU READY TO CHANGE?

Our self-esteem is a state of being, doing, acting, that allows us to appreciate ourselves, and others as valuable, and worthwhile. The person has a positive attitude along with an: I am worthy, I am capable, I am competent, and I can do it belief about themselves and their life. You love yourself; accept you are worthy to exist, have dreams, and have your dreams fulfilled.

There are many kinds of self-esteem, or beliefs you hold about yourself. Sometimes they do not carry over or intertwine in all areas of your life. For example your self-esteem in tennis, will not help you pass an algebra test if you have not studied algebra.

To achieve success in your chosen field, you will need to improve your self-image, and self-worth, to believe you can become a new person with a new profession. Then, practice with your new image, and self-worth until you are comfortable with the new you. The areas of your self-esteem that will challenge you the most, where you will need to work diligently, and be persistent, are with your beliefs, attitudes, acceptance of the new image, and new person you desire to become, and fell worthy and deserving of a greater good.

Your self-esteem is the medium through which you express yourself, to share the divine essence of who you are to the world. When you express from your divine essence it may or may not generate money. However, if what you do is done through a love for mankind, and a desire for God to manifest through you, the universe will compensate you generously. There are many kinds of success, and you can be successful in anything. However if love for others is not a component, it will be a hollow and empty success.

You can do many things to make money, that will lower your self-esteem, rather than elevate it, so you and others feel good about you. For example you can sell cocaine and be a success financially. However, this often involves deceit, contempt for ones fellow man, greed, fears of going to jail, and doing something that violates the rights of society (you do not have the right to use your influence to bring harm to another). Also, anything you do, that you are not proud to share with the world, will negatively affect your self-esteem. This is why many of us have a crippling, self-esteem, that helps us make money but causes us to dislike ourselves, because we are "out of integrity" with ourselves, our fellow man, and life. It is easy to become comfortable with a dysfunctional self-esteem, because we fear change. Often what accompanies change are confusion, anger, blame, and fear of the unknown.

We are such creatures of habits that we long for the familiar; we seek comfort and ease rather than discomfort and distress. Are you ready to change your beliefs, and attitude about whom you will become, to improve your self-esteem? Are you, your family, friends, and significant relationships able to accept a new you? Assess your personal skills to see where you need to improve, or change, to maximize your self-esteem success potential. Are you ready to be your glorious, magnificent self?

ASSESSING MY PERSONAL STRENGTHS

Work, Job, or Position:	**Circle One**
1. I have at least three years work experience.	Yes No
2. I have held a responsible position.	Yes No
3. I enjoy and take pride in my work.	Yes No
4. I get along with my co-workers.	Yes No
5. I feel loyal to my employer or organization.	Yes No

Organizational Strengths:
1. I am able to develop/short-long range goals   Yes No
2. I am able to carry out instructions.   Yes No
3. I am able to give instructions to others.   Yes No
4. I have experience organizing projects/events.   Yes No
5. I am goal oriented, have a sense of direction and purpose in my work and life.   Yes No

Relationship Strength
1. I easily meet people & comfortable with them   Yes No
2. I am polite; I treat people with respect and consideration.   Yes No
3. I am aware of the needs and feelings of others.   Yes No
4. I am able listen intently to what others say.   Yes No
5. I help others be aware of their strengths   Yes No

Special Aptitudes or Resources
1. I have hunches that frequently turn out right, and I follow through on them.   Yes No
2. I am good at my job.   Yes No
3. I am skilled in mathematics   Yes No
4. I have good public relations skills   Yes No
5. I am self motivated.   Yes No

Intellectual Strengths:
1. I use my reasoning ability to problem solving.   Yes No
2. I am curious intellectually.   Yes No
3. I am able to express my ideas, and in writing.   Yes No
4. I am open to new ideas.   Yes No
5. I enjoy learning new things.   Yes No

Emotional Strengths:
1. I am able to give, receive, affection and love.   Yes No

2.	I can feel and express a wide range of emotions.	Yes No
3.	I can do, or express things without hesitation.	Yes No
4.	I have empathy/understand others' feelings.	Yes No
5.	I understand the role of my feelings and emotions at work and at home.	Yes No

My Other Strengths:

1.	I have a good sense of humor and I am able to laugh at myself	Yes No
2.	I like to try new things, and new horizons.	Yes No
3.	I am able to take a risk, grow, and develop my potential.	Yes No
4.	I have perseverance and stick-to-itness.	Yes No
5.	I take care of my health and look my best.	Yes No

PERSONAL STRENGTH ASSESSMENT

Tally your score. Give yourself one point for each **Yes**. There is no optimum number of Yes or No answers. Use this as a tool to notice areas where you are strong or need to improve.

To have a healthy self-esteem you must be: flexible, open to change, able to laugh at your mistakes, creative, continue seeking ways to grow and improve, ask question when you do not understand, give yourself freedom to say no, and yes, take time to pause – catch your breath, and start again.

Listen to your body – understand when it says, take time to smell the roses, meditate, smile, cry, laugh, give thanks to God for blessings received. Remember the highest form of prayer is gratitude.

We wear our attitude outside us. It is written on our face, and broadcasted through our body language. What message are you sending to others about your self-esteem? What is the status of your self-esteem?

SELF ESTEEM ASSESSMENT

1. Who am I? Be specific, avoid global remarks.

2. How I got to be this way

3. What makes me special/unique? Be specific, list five or more traits/characteristics.

4. Attributes or talents I possess.

5. Discovering my talents (things I like to do that are fun and gives me a natural high).

6. My ancestry is special because...

7. Ways I can acknowledge myself without ridiculing others, who look or acts different from me are:

8. Ways I can communicate with others if I am shy or easily embarrassed are:

9. Things I can do to make friends with strangers are:

10. How do I let those of the opposite sexes know I want to be their friend?

11. Things I can do to overcome shame, and embarrassment of myself/family:

12. Since my self-image is an outward projection of my dreams/ desires, I see myself in:

    1 yr . . . .

    5 yrs . . . .

    10 yrs . . . .

13. My old beliefs about me were:

14. My new beliefs about me are:

15. My old attitude about me was:

16. My new attitude about me is:

17. Self-Acceptance is not blinding yourself to your faults, nor hating yourself for them, but claiming, and accepting you can change for the better. And holding to your vision of the new you, even though it may not be apparent to you or anyone. Write what you will do to create a new you below.

   a. My old self-acceptance was:

   b. My new self-acceptance is:

18. My old success self-esteem was:

19. My new success self-esteem is:

DESIDERATA

Go placidly amid the noise and the haste and remember what peace there may be in silence. As far as possible without surrender, be on good terms with all people. Speak your truth quietly and clearly; and listen to others, even to the dull and ignorant; they too have their story. Avoid loud and aggressive persons; they are vexatious to the spirit. If you compare yourself with others, you may become vain or bitter, for always there will be greater or lesser persons than yourself.

Enjoy your achievements as well as your plans. Keep interested in your own career, however humble; it is a real possession in the changing fortunes of time. Exercise caution in your business affairs, for the world is full of trickery. But let this not blind you to what virtue there is ; many persons strive for high ideals, and everywhere life is full of heroism. Be yourself. Especially do not feign affection. Neither be cynical about love; for in the face of all aridity and dis-enchantment, it is as perennial as the grass.

Take kindly the counsel of the years, gracefully surrendering the things of youth. Nurture strength of spirit to shield you in sudden misfortune. But do not distress yourself with dark imaginings. Many fears are borne of fatigue and loneliness. Beyond a wholesome dis-

cipline, be gentle with yourself. You are a child of the Universe no
less than the trees and the stars; you have a right to be here. And
whether or not it is clear to you, no doubt the universe is unfolding
as it should.

Therefore, be at peace with God, whatever you conceive him to be,
and whatever your labors and aspirations in the noisy confusion of
life, keep peace in your soul. With all its sham drudgery, and broken
dreams, it is still a beautiful world.
Be cheerful. Strive to be happy.

AFFIRM FOR YOURSELF
I acknowledge the divine, glorious, magnificent person
that I am. Since I am made in the image, and likeness of God,
I allow this unlimited power to guide and direct my life. I give
up all sense of smallness to express my divine unlimited
potential.

Today I accept all my gifts and talents.
I am amazed how blessed I am.
– DOLLY SEWELL, NOTTINGHAM, ENGLAND

THROUGH OUR DESIRES AND GOALS WE BECOME MOTIVATED TO CHANGE OUR LIVES

1. My 1 year, 5, and 10 year goals in the following areas are: Write **month and year** you will achieve **each goal**

   Personal/Family –

   Education/Study –

   Social/Friendship –

   Spiritual/Religious –

Start now and enjoy the rest of your life. "Life Is Shorter Than You Think."

To Discover Your Career Niche, Ask Yourself These Questions:

1. What things in life give you the greatest pleasure or satisfaction? Write these down then put them in order of #1 greatest satisfaction, #2, etc.

    1.
    2.
    3.
    4.
    5.

    Personal:

    Future Career Goals:

    Social Goals:

    Spiritual Goals:

2. What things do others praise or compliment you on? List them here:

3. Now that you have completed the activities above, *what thing or things* would you enjoy doing every day of the year, even if you were *not paid monetarily?*
   Whatever you choose is your "hot button."

I AM WORTH IT

I may sometime cause confusion when I am unclear in my
  communication, unsure of myself, or uncertain about an
  outcome, yet I am worth the bother.
I may act timid and fearful sometimes, but please remember
  that I am trying to sort things out in my mind, and I am
  worth the bother.
Even though you may struggle to understand me, I am worth it.
My friend, I am the other half of you.
I am incomplete without you, and you are incomplete
  without me.
In some strange way, though we differ in racial composition,
  thoughts,ideas, and behavior; we are wedded to each
  other.
I will release you for now, to soar above the heavens.
Just remember that whatever disappointment or
  challenge I face,
I deserve the best, for I am worth it.
                                   — IDA GREENE

If you believe in yourself and believe in a power greater than yourself, you will achieve success. Since the largest growing population in the United States today is the 85 years and older group, you will journey many times in your lifetime from success to success before you make your transition from planet earth. Often success is the result of patient persistence through failure. So do not become discouraged if you do not see instant results.

We are all a diamond in the rough, becoming our Divine-Self

through our trials and tribulations. Jesus stated "Be of good cheer, for I have conquered the world." You must never quit striving to improve yourself, or your life circumstances, even though you may have challenges, and it takes a long time to reach your goals.

Your success is created from your self expression. And your self-expression is a spiritual quality. You are here in life to express your God potential. Do not confuse your Divine self expression with your livelihood. When you allow God to express through you, all your needs will be met. Never accept a job, or engage in any activity just for money. Because if you do not express your divine, God given talents, you will become disgruntled, bored, and lose enthusiasm for life and living. And when you lose your enthusiasm, you lose your light. Jesus said, " Ye are the light of the world." You are alive, joyous, and aglow when you do work you enjoy, and it fulfills a divine purpose in the universe.

You are a spiritual being, in a human body, having a spiritual experience. Your primary purpose to be on the planet, is to use your divine self expression to grow spiritually, and become a Master like Jesus. We must first master our physical body, before we achieve mastery in our spiritual life. And we do this through right thinking, right living, and right divine self expression. Success is not just about desire, power, and money. It is a spiritual and sacred journey.

Both life and success are about your journey, learned experiences, and personal growth. We grow through each challenge we encounter. No challenge you experience in life will ever leave you where it found you. Each experience teaches us how to be more humble, gentle, loving, compassionate, and how to forgive seventy times seventy. You are here in this life to become your Divine-Self. We become our Christ-Self by listening and responding to the intuition God give us, which is designed to bring forth the divine, and best aspect of our nature so we become God in flesh.

We came from God, and to God we return when we complete our earth's journey. Remember, what you are is God's gift to you. What you make of yourself is your gift to God. Will you return to God the same raw materials given you on your entrance to planet earth; or will you return to God a grand masterpiece. A work of art so magnificent to behold, that all the celestial angels and hosts take a bow. They bow because you fought a good fight. You put your best effort into everything you did. You used your work, creativity, talents, relationships, friendships, and painful life experiences to reach a higher level of service to your fellow man.

We were created to serve and be of service to God through our service to our fellow man. We serve God whenever we serve our fellow man. When we can let go our pride, our prejudice, our possessions, our envy, our jealousy, our hurt feelings, our anger, and our ego; we take on angelic qualities. We become God in the flesh.

You were given dreams, goals, and aspirations to refine your temperament, your spirit, attitude, and to become more loving. Whenever you accomplish any goal, you set out to do, and accomplish it in spite of hardship, or challenge you are a success.

What is success for you, may not be success for another. God speaks to each of us individually. We are each marching to a different drummer.

Success is an inside job. You must first create it within your mind, before it will out picture in the real world of manifestation. And to create it in your mind you must do two things:

1. You must be willing to do whatever is necessary to heal mankind of a belief in separation from each other and God. The universal goal is for us to see ourselves as one. All were created by the One God. There is one energy source, one life, and one Divine Mind, that unites all people as one. We all tap into the same energy source to create prosperity, or anything else. God is the source of all prosperity and abundance.

2. To acquire wealth, or be successful, you must be a larger channel for God to pour through you into the universe. Your goal, is to discover what is your talent, and to find a way to give your gift to the world. *The key to prosperity and abundance is to give.* **"The more you give, the more you get. Give of your time, talent, and treasure."** And be more of a person that someone would want to be with in a business relationship.

Never compare your success or achievements with any other person. Only God alone is the judge, not you or another. For just when you think you have failed, God says, well done my good and faithful servant, you have fought a good fight. You are a success.

The tool you will need to achieve success in anything will be a positive self-esteem anchored in faith. Faith is a positive, mental state of knowing, that even though the outcome may be bleak, look hopeless, and impossible, that the outcome you desire will manifest. Faith is the place where you let go, and grab onto the unknown, which is called God. With faith you have to believe, and know, before it is manifested. Faith is letting Go and letting God, or your higher self take over. The human mind wants to know the outcome before it happens, because we like to be in control of things. If control is your issue, you will have little faith, abundance, prosperity, wealth, or success. *Faith is about being out of control.* It is letting go your control, to discover new horizons, and vistas. It is about gratitude. What can you be thankful for today. The following exercise can help you develop a more positive attitude, which is the foundation for success. Create a daily gratitude list.

I feel good when I think about:

. . . .

. . . .

. . . .

Say To Yourself:: I Affirm

Today I start a new day, a new month, a new year for I am a new me. I accept that I am success, that I am successful in all I do, or will become.

Every day in every way I become better and better and richer and richer

Excellence Has No Fear of Observation

Therefore when you are being your best, it does not matter if others watch you.

The Four-Way Test...of what we think, say or do.

Ask yourself:

1. Is it the *Truth*?
2. Is it *Fair* to all Concerned?
3. Will it Build *Goodwill* and Better Friendships?
4. Will it Be *Beneficial* to All Concerned?

If your answer is yes to all the above, you will be a huge success in your chosen endeavor.

RESPONSIBILITY

1. *Responsibility means accepting the importance of the job we do. Work that we value is the only work that is valuable.*
2. *Responsibility means seeing things from a point-of-view big enough to include the people and the organization around us.*
3. *Responsibility means taking criticism as it is intended: an attempt to improve the quality of our efforts, without ridiculing us as people.*
4. *Responsibility means accepting the little, essential disciplines that go with any team operation – punctuality, neatness safety.*
5. *Responsibility means realizing that the situation at work is like the situation at home – every single thing we do affects someone else, for better or worse.*
6. *Responsibility means accepting problems and difficulties as a normal part of any job. If we had no problems, we would win*

no victories, and without victories, life would be pretty drab.

7. *Responsibility means looking at your complaints to see if they have solutions, or if you're just complaining about things that can't possibly be changed. Complain to someone who can do something to effect the change you want; back room complaints only make everyone unhappy. Be constructive – identify what you see as needing change, and then give positive suggestions about how you think changes can be made.*

    – ANON

AFFIRM

Today there is nothing I can do, say, think, or become that establishes my worth, my self-worth comes from God.

ACCEPT YOUR STRENGTHS AND IMPROVE YOUR WEAKNESS

Place a check by ones you like and circle ones you need to improve.

Improve.	Shy
Confident	Pleasant
Angry	Resourceful
Superior	Secure
Handsome	Kind
Sensitive	Inferior
Planner	Scared
Thoughtful	Bold

117

Argumentative	Selfish
Unfriendly	Giver
Competent	Joyful
Controlling	Insecure
Punctual	Friendly
Bossy	Organized
Smart	Stingy
Creative	

THINGS I WILL CHANGE AS OF TODAY.

I Now Affirm and Accept:

I like me! I like the person I am becoming.
I trust my judgement, and my decision making ability.
I accept that my mind is as good as that of another person.
My mind will work for me and I can make wise decisions.
That I have an excellent memory.
I accept that I am a competent business person.
That I can figure things out with my keen, sharp, mind.
I now release all anger, resentment, and unhappy
thoughts from the past and I am free to soar.
It is O.K. for me to be successful.
It is O.K. for me to be wealthy.
It is O.K. for me to not know everything.
It is O.K. for me to be criticized.
It is O.K. for me to relax, and be myself.
It is O.K. for me to enjoy life, have fun, and love myself.

WINNERS VS. LOSERS

The winner is always a part of the answer;
The Loser is always a part of the problem;
The Winner always has a program;
The Loser always has an excuse;
The Winner says "Let me do It for you;"
The Loser says "That's not my job;"
The Winner sees an answer for every problem;
The Loser sees a problem for every answer;
The Winner sees a green near every sand trap;
The Loser sees two sand traps near every green;
The Winner says "It may be difficult but it's possible."
The Loser says "It may be possible, but it's too difficult."

ARE YOU READY FOR SUCCESS TODAY?

Are you ready for Success? To be successful in any endeavor you must have sales ability. You must be able to sell the greatest commodity in the world, yourself. You will need to be a salesperson, and good sales people are not born, they are created.

The following are traits of top sales people:
1. They have an above average ability and motivation to sell.
2. They are self-starters.
3. They do or act, rather than talk.
4. They enjoy selling.

They may be uncomfortable doing detailed duties, but they are excellent at selling. To be a success in life, you will need to become good at selling. All of life is about selling. And you are the product you will be selling to the world. Learn to esteem yourself daily, to be a better salesperson. To help you in this area, our book *Self-Esteem, The Essence of You – The Milestones of Life* is a good tool to have. Another tool you will need is the ability to manage money and matters related to money. Here is a financial declaration written by Black Enterprise magazine.

DECLARATION OF FINANCIAL EMPOWERMENT

Today is The Day I Take Control of My Financial Destiny. In order to attain a measure of success, power and wealth, I shall uphold the principles of saving and investing as well as controlled spending and disciplined consumerism. I vow to fully participate in the capital markets and make a solid commitment to a program of wealth accumulation. Determination and consistency will serve as my guides, and I will not and cannot allow external or internal forces to keep me from reaching my goals. By adjusting my course and embracing a new mandate that stresses planning, education and fortitude, I lay a strong, unbreakable foundation for the preservation and enrichment of my family, children and children's children.

I (your name) . . . .

from this day forward, declare my vigilant and lifelong commitment to financial empowerment. I pledge the following:

1. *To save and invest 10% to 15% of my after-tax income*
2. *To be a proactive and informed investor*
3. *To be a disciplined and knowledgeable consumer*
4. *To measure my personal wealth by net worth, not income*
5. *To engage in sound budget, credit and tax management practices*
6. *To teach business and financial principles to my children*
7. *To use a portion of my personal wealth to strengthen my community*
8. *To support the creation and growth of profitable, competitive enterprises*
9. *To maximize my earning power through a commitment to career development, technological literacy and professional excellence*
10. *To ensure that my wealth is passed on to future generations*

I have committed to this unwavering, personal covenant as a means of bolstering myself, my family and my community. In adopting this resolution, I intend to use all available resources, wisdom and .power to gain my share of the American Dream.

Agreed and Signed:

. . . .

SAY, YES I CAN!

You are all that the greatest of men have had;
Two arms, two hands, two legs, two eyes,
And a brain to us if you would be wise,
With this equipment they all began.
So start from the top and say, "I can."
Look them over, the wise and the great,
They take their food from a common plate,
And similar knives and forks they use,
With similar laces they tie their shoes,
The world considers them brave and smart,
But you've all they had when they made their start.
You can triumph and come to skill,
You can be great if you only will.
You're well equipped for what fight you choose,
You have arms and legs and a brain to use,
An the person who has risen great deeds to do
Began their life with no more that you.
YOU are the handicap you must face,
You are the one who must choose your place.
You must say where you want to go,
How much you will study the truth to know;
God has equipped you for life, but He
Let's you decide what you want to be.
Courage must come from the soul within

121

The person must furnish the will to win.
So figure it out for yourself, my friend,
You were born with all that the great have had,
With your equipment they all began,
So, Get hold of yourself and say: "I CAN."

— ANON

Both success and money are cyclical. They come and go in cycles. You must remember to never panic when it seems that things are not working as you had planned. Allow the universe and God to make the necessary adjustments which will be in your best interest and that of your business. When you are having a major break through, you sometimes need a break down of your old structure, for the universe to create something new. You greatest enemy will be your fear. We go in depth about how to manage fear in our book Light the Fire Within You. However, remember that whenever you create anything new you will automatically experience a fear of the unknown . You must have a plan of action to help allay your fears. Often a poem, some affirmations or words of inspiration can be useful to help you maintain your focus while you restructure your business or change your direction.

The key is detachment: Avoid holding anything too close to your heart, so that you can let go to start anew, start a new venture or take your business in a new direction.. You may need to relinquish negative or positive feelings,. You will need to relinquish the notion that you are separate from others and relinquish your self will so that a higher power, which I call God can point you in a new direction or set you on a new path. The following are poems to support you on your journey of success.

THE RUGGED ROADS OF LIFE
Life is an ever increasing spiral,
on the path to human perfection.

It matters not the hue of your skin,
>*the color of your eyes, nor the color of your hair.*
For self-mastery is an inner process,
>*that happens each time you overcome an obstacle.*
No one can ever determine,
>*the depth of your learning experience.*
So continue on your journey, to overcome
>*your stiffest challenges,*
For no one will ever know, the depths of your overcoming.
Continue to strive for excellence in every thing you do.
For the path to fulfillment and happiness
>*is the rugged roads of life.*
>>— IDA GREENE

LETTING GO THE PAST

The past as glorious as it was can be better. So let go the tears,
>*old regrets and fears.*
Let go the should, ought to, could have, wish I could have, for
>*it truly is in the past.*
Let go the emotional pain, the sadness, the loneliness, the lack
>*of acknowledgment.*
Today is a new day. It speaks to you of a new dawning.
Today is a new day of hope, possibilities, and potential.

Grab hold of that wish, that desire, that dream, regardless of
>*how small it seems.*
Tuck it deep within your bosom. Let your imagination soar, Let
>*your spirit soar.*
Life is endless. You are eternal. Move through the negativity,
>*the stagnation, and blockage.*

It is time to move. It is time to breathe. It is time to smile. It is
>*time to laugh.*

123

It is time to live. It is time to be. Be the miracle you were des-
   tined to be.
You are good enough. Be whoever you are. Be magnificent, Just
   Be, Just Be. Be....
                    — IDA GREENE

POSITIVE SELF-REGARD AFFIRMATIONS
I behave as an equal to all persons.
I am smart.
I am intelligent.
I am knowledgeable.
I am competent.
I accept my goodness.
I am perfect, just as I am.

DO IT!
Do It! Today is the day, Don't delay.
Do It! This hour is precious, Use it.
Do It! This thought is valuable, Hold it.
Do It! Keep your vision focused up, Keep it.
Do It! This moment is divine, Cherish it.
Do It! The future is now, Embrace it.
Do It! Someday is today, Go for it.
Do It! Greatness is your right, Own it.
Do It! You are Divine, Accept it.
Do It! No one is standing in your way, Move.
Do It! No one will stop you, Go.
Do It! Life is waiting for you to act, Get started.
Do It! This is the life you have been dying to have,
Live it.
Do It! Wealth is your birthright, Claim it.

Do It! Action cures fear, Act now.
Do It! Love is the answer to any problem, Try it.
Do It! God wants to help you, Let go and accept help.
Do It! You are lovely, Be it.
Do It! You are special, Believe it.
— IDA GREENE

THOUGHT FOR THE DAY

Flatter me, and I may not believe you.
Criticize me, and I may not like you.
Ignore me, and I may not forgive.
Encourage me, and I will not forget you.
— ANON

You now have a blueprint for success to follow. Reread this book often. Make notations where needed. Write to tell me of your success stories. Remember if you persist, and are determined to be successful, I will be reading about your accomplishments and achievements in your local newspaper. I wish for you Success, Prosperity, and Peace. I acknowledge you for the contribution you will make to mankind. Go forth in Love, Truth, Justice, aware of your Inner Power, and Presence.

Reread this book often. Make notations where needed. Write to tell me of your success stories. Remember if you persist, and are determined to be successful, I will be reading about your accomplishments and achievements in your local newspaper. I wish for you Success, Prosperity, and Peace. I acknowledge you for the contribution you will make to mankind. Go forth in Love, Truth, Justice, aware of your Inner Power, and Presence.

At People Skills International we work with individuals, and businesses in private consultation on topics of Esteeming Oneself, Empowerment, Motivation, Effective Communication Skills, How To Present Oneself Favorably to Others, Stress Management, How To Light The Fire Within To Become A Better Person, Be More Alive, On Fire, With Drive and Enthusiasm. We have professional and personal development books, that assist people in business or life, they are: Light the Fire Within You, How to be A Success In Business, Soft Power™ Negotiation Skills, Self-Esteem The Essence of You, Say Goodbye to Your Smallness, Say Hello to Your Greatness and Money, How to Get It, How to Keep It. An audio cassette tape album is available on: Light the Fire Within You, Money, How to Get It, How to Keep It, a video and audiocassette on Self-Esteem, The Essence of You. We offer classes on Soft Power™ Negotiation Skills, How To Improve Self-Esteem to Maximize Success, and Success Skills through Personal and Professional Coaching with Dr. Ida Greene at (619) 262-9951 for more information, contact us at www.idagreene.com or E-mail idagreene@idagreene.com

Personal intuitive Coaching is available by phone for a nominal fee, to help you reach your goals. (619) 262-9951 or Fax (619) 262-0505.

BIBLIOGRAPHY

Daily Word, June 1998, Silent Unity, 1901 NW Blue Parkway, Unity Village, Mo 64065-0001.

Holy Bible, King James Version, Penguin Books USA Inc. 375 Hudson Street, New York, New York 10014

Kimbro, Dennis and Hill, Napoleon, *Think and Grow Rich, A Black Choice*, The Napoleon Hill Foundation, Ballantine Books, a division of Random House Inc. 1991

Posner, Mitchell J., *Executive Essentials*, New York: Avon Books, 1987.

Peale, Norman Vincent, *Plus – The Magazine of Positive Thinking*, September 1995

Science of Mind, A Philosophy, A Faith, A Way of Life. Vol. 68, NO 9, (September 1995) Science of Mind Publishing P.O. Box 75127, Los Angeles, CA 90075

Sellers, Reverend, Dr. Delia, Publisher *Abundant Living Magazine*, June 1996, P.O. Box 12525, Prescott, AZ 86304-2525

Printed in the United States
79829LV00002B/352-408

9 781881 165026